COLUMBANUS

Claude LaGrange's 1950 statue of Columbanus at Luxeuil depicting the saint at the moment of his rejection of the royal children of King Theuderic (Courtesy of the Author)

Burnam W. Reynolds
Asbury University, Kentucky

COLUMBANUS
Light on the Early Middle Ages

THE LIBRARY OF WORLD BIOGRAPHY

Edited by: Peter N. Stearns

Boston Columbus Indianapolis New York San Francisco Upper Saddle River
Amsterdam Cape Town Dubai London Madrid Milan Munich Paris Montréal Toronto
Delhi Mexico City São Paulo Sydney Hong Kong Seoul Singapore Taipei Tokyo

Executive Editor: Jeff Lasser
Editorial Project Manager: Rob DeGeorge
Editorial Assistant: Julia Feltus
Senior Marketing Manager: Maureen Prado Roberts
Marketing Assistant: Samantha Bennett
Production Manager: Fran Russello
Art Director, Cover: Jayne Cover
Cover Photo: S. Columbanus (Unsigned by Artist). By permission of Pontifical Irish College, Rome, Italy
Photo Credit: Courtesy of Burnam W. Reynolds
Editorial Production and Composition Service: Murugesh Rajkumar Namasivayam/ PreMediaGlobal
Printer/Binder: Courier Companies, Inc.

Library of Congress Cataloging-in-Publication Data

Reynolds, Burnam W.
 Columbanus: light on the early Middle Ages/Burnam W. Reynolds.
  p. cm. -- (The library of world biography)
 Includes bibliographical references and index.
 ISBN-13: 978-0-321-33889-1 (alk. paper)
 ISBN-10: 0-321-33889-8 (alk. paper)
 1. Columban, Saint, 543-615. 2. Christian saints, Celtic--Biography.
3. Middle Ages. I. Title.
 BR1720.C624R49 2012
 270.2092--dc23
 [B]
                                    2011030061

10 9 8 7 6 5 4 3 2 1

ISBN 10: 0-321-33889-8
ISBN 13: 978-0-321-33889-1

Contents

Editor's Preface

"Biography is history seen through the prism of a person."

—LOUIS FISCHER

It is often challenging to identify the roles and experiences of individuals in world history. Larger forces predominate. Yet biography provides important access to world history. It shows how individuals helped shape the society around them. Biography also offers concrete illustrations of larger patterns in political and intellectual life, in family life, and in the economy.

The Longman Library of World Biography series seeks to capture the individuality and drama that mark human character. It deals with individuals operating in one of the main periods of world history, while also reflecting issues in the particular society around them. Here, the individual illustrates larger themes of time and place. The interplay between the personal and general is always the key to using biography in history, and world history is no exception. Always, too, there is the question of personal agency: How much do individuals, even great ones, shape their own lives and environment, and how much are they shaped by the world around them?

PETER N. STEARNS

Author's Preface

The Irish saint, missionary, and monastic pioneer Columbanus (543–615) is an often-overlooked contributor to Western Civilization. Despite his obscure upbringing and his lifelong call into the self-contained world of monasticism, he was involved in several developments whose effects would ripple across the centuries. He was key to the creation of a unified Western concept of monastic life, and his popularizing of an Irish model of penance has directed the habits of faith for millions down through the centuries. In an age of close interaction between faith and public affairs, the religious changes he participated in were significant for political events as well. It is in part to correct this neglect, and give an important figure of history his proper due, that this work is undertaken.

In his own words, Columbanus came from "the edge of the world," an Ireland just discovering the uses of literacy and ablaze with the intensity of people newly converted to Catholicism. The creative tension that this great flux in Irish society produced contributed much that rejuvenated civilization. Columbanus was to be a harbinger of the movement of Irish scholars and missionaries to the continent.

Columbanus and those who followed his sea path to the European mainland brought a renewed enthusiasm for literacy and religion to societies also experiencing great flux. The post-barbarian invasion realignment of culture, the tentative and shifting configurations of the successor kingdoms of fallen Rome, and the struggle of the Church to process these changes meant that new syntheses were possible. Columbanus participated in the creation of many of these syntheses, sometimes deliberately, sometimes inadvertently by the force of his personality. Along the way, he boldly reprimanded kings, lectured popes, upheld the concept of sanctuary against royal incursion, and enthusiastically, albeit with dubious results, entered into the theological controversies of his day. Through it all he sought to win adherents to his vision of the religious life, even dabbling in the conversion of a pagan people.

While no one person or career can serve as an access point to all, or even most, of the key developments of an era, there are those infrequent lives whose course brings them into contact with many of them. The lives of other giants of this age, Pope Gregory the Great and Boethius to name two of them, are capable of illuminating much of the substance in this transitional age but lack the multiple cultural points of contact and the wide geographic sweep of Columbanus. He was a monk, and by the lights of popular imagination as well as actual practice, he might be expected to remain in one place: his monastery. But Columbanus was a wanderer. During his long and variegated career, he journeyed from his native Irish land, itself a mix of ancient pagan ways and the perspectives of the newly emergent Christianity, to an encounter with the dual milieu of Latin and barbarian cultures. He became, in effect, a man of three cultures, Irish, Latin, and Germanic, who, along the way, was actively involved in the transformation of three of the most influential institutions of the medieval period: the church, monasticism, and kingship.

Therefore, while Columbanus is not the only figure who can serve as a guide to the transition from the Late Antique era to the Middle Ages, his life illuminates this period of change excellently. That is why I have chosen to title this volume *Columbanus: Light on the Early Middle Ages*. The events of his life can serve as a platform upon which the reader might glimpse something of the shift from the last generations of the ancient world to the opening years of a world that was more properly "medieval."

This work intends to be more than a recounting of one man's life, no matter how colorful or arresting that may be. Rather it also uses Columbanus' life to open windows on a world long lost and thereby to illustrate issues such as the blending of Celtic and Benedictine monasticism, the response to the dislocation of society caused by a catastrophic pandemic, and the popularizing of a new form of penance that had long-term political as well as religious implications. Such aspects as the role of the miraculous in medieval life, the interplay of the natural and the supernatural, and the further development of the cult of the saints will inform and shape the story of Columbanus' life.

Historical narrative runs the risk of seeming more objective than it really is, or ever can be. There is no such thing as the simple retelling of the story of a life, for in telling any story there are continual subjective decisions to be made concerning various theories on the actions themselves, their significance, and the matter of selection as to which portions of the tale to highlight or downplay. In Columbanus' case, we have a fair amount of his own work from which we may gain insight into the man. Aside from that, however, additional insight is difficult to extract from these very public writings. As is common in his age, we lack introspective evidence. Early medieval writers focused on actions at the expense of intentions. After Augustine's *Confessions*, written in the early fifth century, one looks in vain for autobiographical explanations of the "why" behind an action. Intentions and motivations are not revealed by Columbanus in spite of the volume of literary evidence he left behind. It should be a simple task to examine the man and his times and yet it is so complex that every version of a life like Columbanus' is the product of numerous subtle choices. It reminds one of the medieval writer Giraldus Cambrensis' assessment of Irish illuminated manuscripts: "The eye will see nothing subtle where everything is subtle." Columbanus' life is only a story, but it is a story made up of countless choices and interpretations. Yet it is a story well worth telling again.

Here I must express my gratitude to all those who have helped me in making this study possible. First I must thank Dr. Peter Stearns, who agreed with my suggestion that Columbanus was worthy of a volume in his series and granted me the opportunity to realize it. I am especially grateful to Jeff Lasser for seeing the book through to completion. All those at Longman, Julia Feltus, Fran Russello, and Cheryl Keenan, in particular, were quite helpful and patient. I am also indebted to the readers of the manuscript, Professors William TeBrake, Deborah Vess, Erika Lindgren, Elizabeth Makowski, Jonathan Scott Perry, Suzanne Balch-Lindsay, and Anders Michael Kinney, who were generous with their time and even more so with their kind remarks. Any deficiencies in the book remain mine alone. Most of all I want to thank my family, especially my son Andrew, and my wife, Machel, who has been a constant encouragement as well as an indefatigable chauffeur as we traveled Columbanus' "life pilgrimage" routes. Without their unwavering support this book never would have happened.

The Measure of the Man

One day in the year A.D. 590, a boat hove into view off the western coast of France. It most likely was a curragh, a wooden-framed, hide-covered sea vessel of Irish provenance, and it contained thirteen passengers. They were a strange-looking lot, wan from self-denial with tattooed eyelids, their heads shaved in front up to the crown, and their hair flowing long behind as was their monastic custom. Each carried his meager possessions and was fully aware that he would never return to his homeland again. The leader of this band, a man approaching fifty, was Columbanus. He would become an apostle of change: the leading edge of a wave that would fully break over the continent during the next century.

From the northeastern corner of Ireland and the thriving monastic settlement of Bangor just outside modern Belfast, they had made their way over the turbulent Irish Sea out into the blustery Atlantic and then eastward to Brittany on the coast of Gaul. A journey such as this would frequently be fatal in a world lacking meteorological predictions and seaworthy crafts. The historical records cannot show how many merchants, pilgrims, and even armies were lost when trying the uncertainties of the sea. Those who survived often sank into the same unrecorded anonymity as those who perished. Why should this little band be any different, and why should they be remembered even today?

For years historians have argued over this perplexing question: Does the person make history, or does history make the person? As with most either/or questions in the study of the past, the correct answer might actually be "Both." For there are identifiable moments where the individual just happened to be in the right place at the right time to affect history and there are others, far fewer it would seem, where an individual by the force of his personality, talent, or sheer will turned events in a specific direction. It seems to be a matter of preponderance—was it more the situation or more the person who determined the historical outcome? Occasionally, although rarely, one person so shapes an era that it is forever linked in the historical imagination with his or her personal history. These rare individuals are much more than a particle in a larger mass; they are the catalyst that moves the human story in a completely new and pervasively important direction. For example, one can think of the career of Alexander the Great and his role in forming the Hellenistic Age, or Martin Luther's own private convictions that set in motion what would become the Protestant Reformation.

There are other eras, or other alterations in the course of history, that are not quite so apparent, or as stark, as these, yet attributable to a key person just the same. Perhaps one such juncture is in the shift from the ancient world to what may properly be termed the Early Middle Ages. For this transition, one compelling figure is the wandering Irish monk Columbanus (543–615). By the strength of his personality, the novelty of his ideas, and the faithful continuation of these by his disciples, he assisted in a redirection of Western Civilization from the ancient world to the beginnings of an era that was truly medieval. In so doing he participated in the blending of Greco-Roman culture with that of the barbarian north, thereby playing a role in the creation of a new European civilization that persists in an identifiable form to this very day.

One thing that makes Columbanus' place in history worth a reexamination is the current state of the study of the sixth and seventh centuries. Traditional historians believed that the obvious break between the ancient world and the Early Middle Ages was the fall of the Roman Empire to the various barbarian invaders of the fifth century. This view was typified in the epic work of the French historian Ferdinand Lot (1866–1952), who titled his book on the barbarian invasions *The End of the Ancient World and the Beginning of the Middle Ages*. Yet the great Belgian historian Henri Pirenne (1862–1931) noticed that the real break with the ancient world might have come in the eighth century. The completion of the Muslim conquest of the southern Mediterranean coastlines, such as North Africa and most of Spain, effectively completed by the 730s, as well as the emergence of Charlemagne's court in the northern portions of what was to become "France" (the term *Francia*, or "land of the Franks," was replacing Gaul as the designation of choice) might provide a surer breakpoint than even the barbarian invasions of the fifth century. Pirenne therefore suggested that the Middle Ages might have begun in the late eighth century, rather than with the fall of Rome three centuries earlier. The further studies by specialists on Rome, such as Chester G. Starr (1914–1999), argued that Rome itself was becoming more and more "barbarized" in its last centuries so that the Late Empire was increasingly seen as indistinguishable from the barbarian generations that followed Rome's fall. Both perspectives tended to lessen the transformational impact of the barbarian invasions of the fifth century.

By the 1970s, scholars, led by the brilliant Peter Brown, were recompartmentalizing the ancient and medieval eras. Now a period known as Late Antiquity (c. A.D. 250–750) that encompassed the last centuries of the Roman Empire and the opening centuries of the postinvasion age was in place. The Early Middle Ages were seen to begin with the Carolingians in the eighth century and thereafter. Historians began to speak of a "Carolingian Renaissance," and ascribe to Charlemagne the creation of a truly European civilization that would emerge to replace the "sub-Roman" barbarian world. Certainly these designations are somewhat artificial, since there is much more continuity than breakage between eras, and many still ably defend the fifth-century fall of Rome as the key turning point. Yet this reordering of the chronological terminology of the Middle Ages brings us face-to-face with the one man who had much to say about shaping the Early Middle Ages, as distinct from Late Antiquity: Columbanus.

Statue of Columbanus at his foundation of Luxeuil. The plaque at the base describes him as "the savior of civilization" and credits him with bringing a presence "like a radiant sun on all the early middle ages."

But how was this wanderer from the edges of the-then civilized world instrumental in the ushering in of a new age? The ideas he brought were not new to his native soil, but they caused great strain and change in the lands he visited. He is sometimes credited with too much, as attested by the modern statue at his monastery in Luxeuil that commemorates him as *le saveur de la civilization*, ("the savior of civilization"). This is certainly an exaggeration, since the same texts and tools of learning that were available to Columbanus back in Ireland were equally available on the continent. The relative level of barbarity, perhaps more noticeable in Gaul, was not markedly different in Ireland. He was no "savior" coming from a brighter place to illuminate a dreadfully benighted corner. But the fact that he could be considered seriously as a savior of civilization at all is indicative of the significant power of his legacy.

One of his contributions was to reinterpret civilization in a fashion that would enable both Roman and barbarian sectors of society to find a common ground. In so doing, he helped to prepare the blending of disparate cultures into one, which is why many consider him to be "the first true European." Originally a Greek word meaning "one who speaks nonsense syllables" rather than Greek, the term *barbarian* became a common descriptor to differentiate those in the civilized world of Rome from the largely tribal peoples beyond the Empire's borders. Owing to the increasing military tension along those borders, there was a general love-hate relationship between the two categories of people, barbarian and Roman. The fourth-century Roman law collection known as the Theodosian Code made certain barbarian customs and costume illegal, while cultured Romans such as Ausonius lamented the growing popularity of barbarian dialects in Gaul. Yet Rome increasingly relied on barbarian troops to defend her borders against other, hostile tribes. In that same fourth century so many Germanic warriors were employed as *federati*, or allied Roman troops, that the word *barbarus* became synonymous with *soldier*. Even after the invasion period subsided, the cultural tension remained. The sixth-century Synod of the Grove of Victory prescribed "penance for the remainder of his life" for anyone who had betrayed Christians to barbarians, while the Penitential of Cummian (c. 650) also used the word *barbarian* to describe the invaders of Western Europe. Even though cultural blending was well underway, there was still much work to be done to meld these two ethnic and cultural categories. In a world where the concept of "the personality of the law," or the existence of separate laws and customs for barbarian and Roman subjects, held sway, Columbanus would facilitate an eventual unity, if not in law itself, at least in the common denominator of church practice.

But do not interpret whatever unity he may have fostered as accommodation. Whatever Columbanus' impact, it was not the product of amiable negotiation, but of confrontation, challenge, and stony resolution. The courage of his convictions could border on rashness. His was a personality capable of defying his beloved mother in order to follow what he believed to be the call of God. He did not shrink from confronting kings and queens, telling them in no uncertain terms of their faults both spiritual and political. He stormed into the midst of a wild, pagan reverie and smashed their ceremonial beer cask to bits. He wrote popes in a tone alternately conciliatory and condescending and lectured assembled bishops on their correct function. Everywhere he went his presence was felt in a memorable and often unpleasant way. He was called *Scottius iracundus* ("irascible Irishman"), for good reason. Yet for all his intensity, it was said that he could be gentle and charismatic. Squirrels frolicked around his shoulders as he read in the quiet of a forest glen, and barbarian nobles were so impressed by his fatherly qualities that they willingly entrusted their sons to him for instruction.

Columbanus was not an easy person with whom to deal. Yet this irascible Irishman to all he encountered left scores of disciples who dotted the landscape of Europe with monastic islands of learning. These foundations helped to set the stage for the Carolingian glory of the subsequent century, and transformed the way Christian Europe regarded the essentials of worship, resulting in a vastly different religious and political path for Western Civilization. In many ways his career assisted the beginning of a new era in Europe. But who was this man, really?

The Overshadowed Man

Oddly enough, for a man who had such influence on Western Civilization, Columbanus is often overlooked entirely or confused with someone else. He is not even mentioned in the Irish annals, perhaps because most of his stellar career was spent abroad on the continent. But this does not explain the omission of his many early accomplishments in learning and monastic administration while at one of the most famous of all Irish monasteries: Bangor. The great early twentieth-century scholar of sixth-century Ireland, Helena Concannon, went out of her way to rationalize this neglect by theorizing that Columbanus' deeds were mistakenly ascribed to others with similar names. There were many Irish churchmen named *Colm*, or "dove," just as this Columbanus.

So what can we know and what can we surmise about this individual and his accomplishments? As with virtually all subjects of this era, we are somewhat at a loss for information on Columbanus and his inner workings. The sources will not permit it, even though he left behind a series of letters, sermons, poems, a penitential, and a rule for monks. Even though he reveals little or no awareness of his own role for Western Civilization as a whole, perhaps we are able to see with the clarity provided by distance and the passage of time what he could not. So it may be with Columbanus and his contribution to the formation of our Western culture out of the fire and gravel of postinvasion Europe. It all began, oddly enough to our ears, with a dream.

The Dream and the Birth

The story begins in the southeastern corner of Ireland, by many accounts the sunniest and driest of that storied isle, where under the shadows of the Blackstairs Mountains, a young woman was expecting her first child. It was the year 543. One evening, perhaps in the last uncomfortable months of pregnancy, while in a fitful slumber, she dreamed that something resembling a sun rose from her womb and went forth to light up the whole world. While we today might discount such a dream as the unwelcome by-product of indigestion, or some strange subconscious rearrangement of the fragments of the day's events, the people of the sixth century believed rather consistently that dreams had strong prophetic power, even if they appear to us as later constructed literary devices intended to validate the subject's status. Columbanus is often depicted iconographically as bearing a sun on his chest, an obvious allusion to his mother's dream, while the same inscription at Luxeuil that hails him as the savior of civilization also mentions his bringing light to a dark region with a radiance like the sun. The sun imagery of Columbanus' birth dream informed his legacy down to recent times, but was not exclusive to him alone.

This construct was particularly popular in Ireland. St. Finnian of Clonard (d. 548) was said to have had a dream in which his two finest pupils, Columba of Iona and Ciaran of Clonmacnoise, were seen as moons of gold and silver, respectively. The golden one, Columba of Iona, lighted the northeastern portion of Ireland and even the lands that would be Scotland, while the silver moon of Ciaran lit up the whole center of Ireland. This dream was confirmed by the actual deeds of these two men: Columba did found the great monastic center at Iona and convert the Picts, while Ciaran established the monastery of Clonmacnoise on the central Shannon River to illuminate spiritually the midlands of Ireland. Ciaran's own mother was said to have received word of a dream had by a holy bishop that her little son would shine as "the sun shineth among the stars of heaven." St. Enda, whose monastery in the western Aran Islands would be a cradle of saints, was portrayed as dreaming that one of his pupils would be like a great tree growing up in the center of Ireland to shelter the nation. The birth of another St. Ciaran, called Ciaran of Saighir to differentiate him from the famous Ciaran of Clonmacnoise, was supposedly foretold by his mother dreaming a star fell into her mouth while she slept thereby producing the baby saint.

But dreams were not always used as constructed literary predictions of greatness. On the continent, in the Loire Valley of France at the city of Tours, Bishop Eufronius was visited in a dream by two holy women martyrs, Saints Maura and Britta, who complained to him about the poor condition of their gravesites. After repeated admonitions from the spirits, Eufronius finally organized a building party to locate their resting places and construct suitable prayer chapels over their remains. Sometimes these "corrective" dreams could get physical. In 697, St. Adamnan, who would gain fame as the biographer of one of Ireland's key saints, was visited in a dream by an angel who demanded that he push for church legislation protecting women in warfare. Apparently Adamnan seemed reluctant, so the angel repeatedly struck him on his side with a staff until the bruised Adamnan finally promised to obey. Days later, at the Synod of Birr, the battered Adamnan produced what has ever since been called the *Lex Innocen-*

A standard depiction of Columbanus shows him with a sun emblazoned on his chest;
a clear reference to his mother's dream just before his birth. This later medieval statue
features him in this fashion.

tium, or "Law of the Innocents," which attempted to limit the ferocity of war by making women and other noncombatants off limits to marauding armies.

Even kings, whether righteous or not, could be visited by these prophetic dreams. Leovigild, who reigned as King of Visigothic Spain from 568 to 586, was a staunch Arian, holding that God the Father, Son, and Holy Ghost were not in existence from the beginning of eternity, as the Trinitarian view maintained, and that Christ was at some point created. Leovigild was so firm in his belief that he persecuted the Trinitarian Christians, even sending a leading bishop, Masona of Merida, into forced exile because he would not conform. Shortly thereafter, the king was visited in a dream by St. Eulalia who beat him with whips until he promised to relent. Dreams of this stripe were very serious indeed, often seeming to leave tangible scars of their visitation.

Dreams like these may seem odd to us today but were a logical function of a society that saw no real separation between the natural and the supernatural. There was a union of the two, allowing the dead to speak rather freely with the living. One Frankish king, Chilperic (r. 561–584), actually placed a letter on the tomb of St. Martin of Tours and came back the next day expecting a written reply from the long-dead saint. It was believed that the supernatural world could speak to the living to foretell greatness, instruct as to proper behavior, or even settle court cases. This became one of the fundamental underpinnings of the trial by ordeal, widely used to determine guilt or innocence.

But something can be common and still be exceptional. What may seem to us to be an abundance of such prophetic dreams were still considered a special and highly significant occurrence. Not just anyone could be visited in this way, nor be the subject of such a visitation. It is part of the tension of the sixth and seventh centuries that Church officials contended with the theologically untrained, "common" believers over whose dreams may be trusted. It was not a matter of rank, or status, but purity of heart that validated the dream. The Frankish King Chilperic did not receive an answer to his letter placed on the dead saint's tomb because he was considered an "impious" man by the clergy. Yet the poorest of the poor might receive a dream of instruction from the supernatural world of faith if their hearts were righteous. So when a young mother in the rural reaches of Ireland was said to have had a dream in which her unborn son would illuminate the world like the sun itself, the public would see it as a special anointing from God.

The Problem of Hagiography

But did that dream, and its special anointing, actually happen or was it added in later to expand the legend of a man as significant as Columbanus? As with much in these centuries and certainly much that deals with our subject, the quality of the sources is essential to the validity of the story itself. Our source for Columbanus, apart from his own writings, which reveal virtually nothing about his early years, is a monk who wrote nearly thirty years after Columbanus' death. He was Jonas of Susa, so named after his home town in the Italian

Alps, but he is known to posterity as Jonas of Bobbio since his career largely revolved around his time at Columbanus' monastery of Bobbio in Lombardy. As he was writing in c. 642/643 about Columbanus, who died in 615, we may suspect that much hearsay had already been turned into legend. Yet a biography written less than three decades after its subject's demise is a reasonably near one in ancient and medieval terms. The earliest account of Alexander the Great, for example, was written more than three centuries after his death, and most medieval saints' lives were written long after the subject's demise. But relative chronological nearness is no guarantee of accuracy. Even those life stories of Christian saints written soon after their passing may be suspected of embellishment in order to establish the saint's holiness among the public. The prototype of this genre is the *Life of St. Martin* by Sulpicius Severus, written only twelve or thirteen years after Martin's death on November 8, 397. So Jonas' *Life of Columbanus* was not exceptional in its timing, at least in Christian literary circles, but may have other problems of accuracy.

The real problem with Jona's *Life of Columbanus* is not the date of its composition or even its general factuality. He apparently conducted extensive interviews with Attala, the abbot who succeeded to Columbanus' leadership at Bobbio upon the saint's death, and even journeyed to Luxeuil in France to interview the abbot at the saint's main early monastic foundation. It was eyewitness accounts and the observations of close friends and colleagues that went into the making of this *Life*. The problem, however, is not with the facts but with the selection and interpretation of the facts. The *Life of Columbanus*, our main source, is not a biography as we might understand it, but belongs to a style of writing called *hagiography*, or "holy writing." It may look like a biography, but its intent is quite different. Biographies seek to describe and explain the events of a person's life with the intention of showing the reader the characteristics and strengths of the human subject. Hagiography intends to use the events of a human life in order to illustrate how God worked through humans. The key word in the sixth and seventh centuries is the Latin word *virtus*. On the surface it looks like our modern word *virtue*, but it actually means something like "holy deeds." It is not a thing that a person has, such as virtue, but something God displays through him or her. The focus is on God, not man. Consequently details that are not useful in showing God's power are omitted as unnecessary. The very things that would make Columbanus human to us are often left out because they did not serve the reason for his life to be recorded.

How does this hagiographic style actually play out in the case of Columbanus? Who was this baby boy whose birth required announcement by such a portent? To begin, we don't know Columbanus' mother's name or that of his father. The father appears nowhere in the story and no clue is given as to his fate. The mother is depicted only as the recipient of the prophetic dream and later as an obstacle to the fulfillment of Columbanus' true calling in life. These mysterious omissions have long puzzled scholars. One theory, popular in the early twentieth century, was that Jonas knew no Irish and so avoided mentioning any complex Irish names. This was also used to explain why no mention was made of Columbanus' exact birth site as well as his family or clan affiliation—a point of great importance in sixth-century Ireland. While this is plausible, it is more likely that the information was excluded because it was of little or no significance in telling the story of how God used the saint. This is a common perspective in saints' lives.

It also affects the location of Columbanus' birth date. No precise date is given and estimates fluctuate between 540 and 550. The year 543 is the most popular guess, owing to one of Columbanus' poems, written shortly before his death in November 615, in which he alludes to the fact that he is seventy-two years old. Even then, the month and day are beyond our knowing. But in the fifth through the seventh centuries the day of a saint's birth was not the important date, but the day of his or her death. This day, when the saint went to heaven, was the official date for the saint's festival. While this may seem backward to us, it made good sense to the masses in Europe to emphasize something other than the date of physical birth. The Roman funerary inscription practice that marked the lifespan of the deceased by how many years, months, and days they lived was based on relative chronology. This involved the description of the length of life rather than its exact location in the commonly accepted year. This was still in force when the saint cults first began to flourish. But with the saints, whose entry into heaven was considered of paramount importance, an absolute chronology was necessary—at least for their death day. In spite of this, the general atmosphere was one that deemphasized the day of birth. For saints, or future saints, the day of death was all that really mattered.

This also poses problems for Columbanus' name itself. We are at a loss as to whether "Columbanus" was his birth name. The name means "dove," so it is thought that he was given this name by his adoring mother who could liken her little baby to a gentle dove. Yet this seems out of step with Columbanus' career. His later personality was anything but like a cooing, peaceful dove. A man so confrontational and aggressively bold would carry the moniker "dove" absurdly. In a letter to Pope Boniface, written in the last year of his life, he seems to hint that his name was a gift from his mother, referring to it as a "birth-right," but the context is somewhat unclear. If not named at birth, when would he be named? There is traditional evidence that young men who became monks in Ireland often forsook their given names and took new monastic ones. St. Patrick himself was originally named *Sochet* ("good at war") until he took his famous Christian name, and St. Columba of Iona was said to have been named *Crimthain* (or "Crimmon," which means "fox"), before he entered the monastery.

If Columbanus were named something else, and deliberately took the name *dove*, it would still seem quite a misnomer given his personality. But, if the name were taken later in life, he may have chosen it with a different meaning in mind. Doves were the traditional symbol of the Holy Spirit in Christian iconography and scripture. However, the Holy Spirit was not always seen as a gentle, passive bird but also as tongues of fire. Columbanus may have felt his mission in life was to purify a society that had become lax and corrupt using the white-hot flame of controversy and confrontation. His name may have signified his peculiar theological interpretation more than some happenstance of naming by a doting mother.

One more point concerning Columbanus' name is its commonness. There were many Irish monks named Colm. This could mean it was a common name for Irish baby boys in general, or for young monks in particular. While there were scores of Columbas and Columbanuses and at least sixty Saint Cormacs, some fourteen St. Brendans, and not less than twenty St. Ciarans, each was given some kind of territorial or occupational designation to separate each one from others. Our Columbanus receives no such special differentiation. While he might have been called "the Missionary," or "the Pilgrim," due to his life of wandering and founding monasteries, the very itinerant nature of his career meant that he could not be called St. Columbanus of any one particular place.

In fact, Columbanus is often in the shadow of Columba of Iona (521–597), a man some twenty years his senior whose flamboyant career encompassed the founding of the great monastic center at Iona (or *insula*, "island"—eventually morphing into "Iona") and the conversion of the Picts. This man's career, which involved both the first recorded sighting of the Loch Ness monster and the first official consecration, as opposed to a mere baptism, of a barbarian king (Brude MacMaelgwyn, King of the Picts), was well recorded in Irish annals. But how could Columba and Columbanus be confused? Both men were called in their native Irish, *Colm*. To differentiate the two, Colm of Iona was called "Columba," while the Colm who is the subject of this biography was called "Columbanus," both Latin versions of "dove." Even today people still confuse Columbanus with Columba when asked about this subject.

We are, however, certain that this baby boy, who would become a wanderer and would affect the history of many nations, was born in the kingdom of *Coiced Laigin*, or Leinster, in the southeastern quadrant of the island of Ireland, somewhere between the Rivers Slaney and Barrow, perhaps on or near the modern border between Counties Carlow and Wexford. The real question, once again unanswered by our sources, is how Columbanus became Christian. It appears that he was raised in the Christian faith as there is no indication that he had a religious conversion experience at any point in his life. He is portrayed by Jonas as a pious young man who needed only a slight provocation to take the step away from being merely a regular believer to the radical commitment to becoming a monk. It is, however, a common construct of hagiography to portray the adult saint as possessing a youthful inclination to intense religion. But the implication is that if Columbanus were raised a Christian—no sure thing in the first century after the landing of St. Patrick—his family must have already been Christian.

Baptism of a Saint

If that is true, then we may surmise some things about Columbanus. First, as a baby born to Christian parents in 543, he would have likely been baptized soon after birth. Back in 407, Pope Innocent I (r. 401–417) had agreed with the arguments of the great North African churchman St. Augustine (354–430) that the doctrine of original sin whereby Adam's fall in the Garden of Eden had corrupted the entire subsequent human race with an inclination toward sinning, required that babies be baptized quickly so that if they died, they would not be condemned to hell. This harsh view was said to have been the product of Augustine's observing a young nursing mother who, when she took her little baby from her breast, caused the infant to fly into a rage. Augustine reasoned that babies, innocent as they may seem, had within them, as does all mankind, the tendency to sin. The result of this was that after the pope's decree of 407, all children born to Christian parents were to be baptized as quickly as possible to protect them from hell. With infant mortality so high, this was the accepted course of action. On the continent the rapid baptism of infants was already deciding their names, for babies baptized on a particular saint's feast day were often named after that saint. This practice continued for centuries. Martin Luther, born late at night on November 10, 1483, was baptized the next day, November 11, and named Martin because November 11th was St. Martin of Tours' feast day. The Ireland of Columbanus' day was not yet taken by these saints' feast days, being so new to the practice of the faith and so much on the periphery of the Christian world. Therefore, we have no evidence that Columbanus was named after a saint, if in fact this name was even given to him at birth. We may say, however, that he was in all probability baptized very soon after his arrival into the world.

It appears that the custom in his day was to baptize the baby eight days after its birth, a parallel to the Old Testament timing for circumcision. We cannot be sure of the exact ceremony, but the later work called the *Stowe Missal*, spells out the proper form in minute detail. The baptism, done in the name of the Father, Son, and Holy Ghost, the so-called triple immersion, was intended to drive out the Evil One "from the head, the hairs of the head, and its crown, from the brain and the forehead, from the eyes, and ears, and nostrils, from the mouth and tongue, and the part under the tongue." The litany would then proceed to enumerate in this fashion most of the significant parts of the body, and some not so significant, before concluding with an all-encompassing finale: "From the thoughts, and the words, and the works, and from all his conversations, now and to come." Baptism was indeed a serious and complete endeavor, and little Columbanus was, owing to his family's Christianity, no doubt washed in the baptismal font with a ceremony somewhat like this.

The Early Years

We may also assume that this little baby would be brought up in a home that valued the ability to read. Christianity had come to the general populace of Ireland with the coming of St. Patrick in 432. While Patrick receives most of the credit in the heavily legend-encrusted accounts, the conversion of Ireland was not his accomplishment alone but due to a legion of unnamed missionaries who spread that faith throughout the island in the late fifth and early sixth centuries.

Christianity brought as a central requisite the idea that a true follower of the faith should be literate enough to read the Bible and the ever growing number of devotional and liturgical works. The biblical books and inspirational texts of this developing Christian tradition were written in Greek and Latin. The Irish had a rudimentary form of written communication called *Ogam* (named after their god of knowledge, *Ogmios*) but mostly experienced their rich tradition of storytelling in oral form. The keepers of this knowledge often trained for as much as two decades before successfully committing the huge body of lore to memory. With the coming of Christianity and its emphasis on literacy, the Irish began to devise their own writing system and transcription of their cultural heritage. Literacy was becoming an increasingly attractive attribute, particularly in a Christian homestead. While literacy was in a demonstrable decline on the continent, in the Ireland of Columbanus' day there was an efflorescence of writing. Ireland was not completely Christianized by the mid-sixth century, but this little baby Columbanus would, by virtue of the accident of his birth to a Christian family in a society discovering that faith and its emphasis on literacy, be placed on a path that could just as easily lead to church service as to a place in secular society.

But what type of society, whether Christian or pagan, might this be? While the details of Columbanus' early years are either missing entirely from his own writings and Jonas' *Life*, or very sketchy in nature, we may be able to grasp something of the origins of the mature, famous man by examining what we know of the world in which he was born and raised.

2

The World of His Youth

It has been said that we are all children of our times, despite our persistent conceit that some are in advance of their times. But it may be said with equal or better accuracy that we are all in some measure a product of the place where we are born and raised. The times and place shape, to a significant degree, the person and form a stage upon which the life is played out. When cultural customs are added to the physical surrounding a matrix that shapes the beliefs and personality of its progeny is formed.

In order to capture the essence of the world into which Columbanus came, we must enter with our imaginations an Ireland long lost. Much of the basic topography of the land remains the same today: Mountain ranges ring the coasts, and multiple rivers, lakes, and bogs appear in the interior. Its mild climate (infrequent and light snows in the winter, wet and windy summers in which the temperature rarely exceeds the seventies) is also unchanged since the sixth century, nurturing the verdant vegetation that has given the island its nickname of *The Emerald Isle.* But much was quite different as well. Where today there are rolling fields of that signature Irish green, in the sixth century there was dense forestation. Travel was possible by means of the river network, making goods and materials at least three times cheaper to move in this way than by land. Land travel was restricted largely to the occasional gravel ridge, called eskers, left over from ancient glacial action and beaten clean by the countless footfalls of men and beasts as well as supplemented by the laying of rough wooden planking to shore up the points where bogs or too deep dales broke the path. Ireland was bisected into northern and southern halves. The north was called in the ancient sources *Leth Cuinn* or "Conn's Half," and the south the *Leth Moga* ("Mog's Half"). The island's ancient trackways reinforced this with a major route running from modern-day Dublin all the way west to Galway Bay. The Shannon River divided the country on an east-west axis, connecting upstream on its 220-mile extent from the Atlantic to the lakes of northwestern Ireland. This river, like others of the island, tended to flood easily over its low banks during the heavy rains of winter, creating a flood plain along its course called "the Callows," which in summer became a verdant grassland. It was an agrarian world, much attuned to the rhythms of nature and often imprisoned by their requirements. The countryside was fragrant with the smell of woodsmoke and freshly turned earth. Stock raising, particularly cattle and pigs, was a typical sign of wealth.

Bucolic as this may seem, the Ireland of the sixth century sheltered a population that was isolated generally in homesteads, or *duns*, containing the extended family, or *fine*. Despite the seeming isolation, it was a society capable of cultural shifts and interpenetration as witnessed by the spread of an entirely new religion, Christianity, in only a century. This is no mean feat in a society such as this that is based on traditional custom and it speaks volumes of the

Map 2.1 The Ireland of Columbanus' Youth

early Irish willingness to consider new ideas. It was also an Ireland of petty kingdoms: the stitching together of clans and homesteads into a primitive fabric of government. The sixth century would see not only the adoption of a new religion but also a major reshuffling of power leading to the earliest emergence of what would later be the dominant royal force in Ireland: the Uí Neill. The old divisions of Ulster in the north, Connaught in the west, Munster in the southwest, Leinster in the southeast, and *Mide* (Meath) in the eastern center would continue to exist, but in an increasingly jeopardized form during the coming centuries. The era of Columbanus' birth was a time of greater-than-usual turmoil and danger in which the family association, and its homestead, or *dun*, would be even more important than before. In this age, lacking a central authority with neither police nor army to protect the citizens, the fine, or family was the only means of support and protection.

Columbanus is thought to have begun his life on one of these homesteads. Once again information on its exact nature is lacking. We cannot say which dun was his birthplace, for many of the hundreds of homesteads did not survive the centuries to become the villages of modern Ireland. Today the village of Bunclody is the nearest town of any size to the probable birth site. It appears his birth dun was in the vicinity of Mt. Leinster, the highest peak in the Blackstairs Mountains towering nearly half a mile into the air. This is significant in that Columbanus' great monastic foundations on the continent would also nestle near mountain ranges, first in the Vosges of eastern France and second in the Cottian Alps in northern Italy. It seems that the man did not wander far from his home topography even when he found himself in a far distant land.

Family Ties

Some scholars have conjectured that his family was quite well-to-do, owing to his early access to training and the privileges that go with it. Some have even tried to affiliate him with the Fothairt clan, a prominent family in the Leinster of his era. We simply cannot know, although it may be accurate to say that Columbanus' family was not too highly placed among the nobility of that day because he apparently was not subject to the old Celtic custom of fosterage, where young noble boys would be sent to be raised by another, well-connected family as a means of creating alliances. Columbanus seems to have spent his formative years at his own homestead.

How might that homestead have appeared? Apart from the surrounding pasturage and tilled fields, the habit of digging a protective ditch, perhaps topped with sharpened wooden stakes, encircling the dun was already commonplace in the sixth century. This boundary, called the *les*, was protective to be sure but also marked off the area reserved for the fine and was private to outsiders unless given permission to enter. Within the les, Columbanus may have lived in what we today would classify as a hut. The sixth century throughout Europe was a very shrunken world with little in the way of spacious living structures. The less square footage and the smaller the windows and doors the less heat loss on a cold night. The house would often be of wattle and daub construction: branches woven around and over poles to form an inner and outer wall which would then be daubed inside and out with river clay mixed with cattle dung or straw as a binding agent. The space between the double walls would be stuffed with rags or straw or any other suitable insulating material, with the roof thatched and holding a small hole to let out the smoke from the fire kept burning on the interior hearth. A drainage ditch would be dug around the base of the hut to keep the heavy rainwater from turning the beaten dirt floor into a muddy morass. Perhaps Columbanus' home was a bit more sturdy in that it might have been constructed of the endless limestone rocks turned up in field plowing which made dry stone masonry buildings as well as rock walls possible throughout Ireland.

As a little boy Columbanus would have had the run of the homestead, and with the extended family living there too, plenty of cousins or other relatives as companions. The custom of the times, as outlined by the ancient Brehon Laws, seems to indicate that those of a highly placed free status wore clothing of distinctive colors, red, green, and brown, as a mark of their rank in society. Linen clothes, the brownish flax bleached white in the sun after soaking in urine, were also the mark of the wealthy. Columbanus would have been no pale, indoor lad. He was reputed to have grown to be blond, muscular, and well schooled in the arts of outdoor life. Irish boys training for a life of leadership in the clan were expected to be proficient in horseback riding, even including a leaping mount, shooting the bow, and athletic feats with warlike usefulness such as throwing stones, jumping for height, and undergoing flexibility training. The young Columbanus would also no doubt be skilled in the use of the Irish axe. Aside from clearing brush, shaping building materials and the like, this one-handed axe, somewhat akin to the Frankish one on the continent, was used as a throwing weapon in warfare. Columbanus' later life indicates that he learned valuable lessons as a boy in the art of wilderness survival: knowing edible from poisonous plants, how to track through a forest, how to find water and how to construct a serviceable shelter, and even how to select a commanding house site. All these skills, learned in the woods and fields of Leinster, would serve him very well in his adult journeys and at his monastic foundations.

The Question of Education

Yet all these competencies were complemented, and therefore reinterpreted, by another training only recently accepted in Irish culture: literacy. The Irish had always cherished the stories of their gods, heroes, and ancestors but these were oral traditions handed down after prodigious feats of memorization by specially anointed bards. Now with the appearance of Christianity, a "religion of the book," the ability to read and write became essential in preparing a young man for leadership both secular and sacred. It was not just for clerics that literacy was becoming essential, but society as a whole was being leavened by the written word, as ancient laws and customs were recorded in a newly created script. Columbanus was certainly prepared in this way. We know for a fact that Columbanus was literate when he entered the monastery in his teen years. The real question is how he became educated.

While Jonas of Bobbio is maddeningly silent on particulars about Columbanus' early life, including his education, we do know that other, contemporary religious leaders were educated before they entered the monastery. St. Ciaran of Clonmacnoise was taught to read and write by a priest or a deacon, while St. Columba of Iona was instructed by a bard who had become Christian. We have no clue as to who taught the young Columbanus; it could have been a local priest or a hired tutor, or even his own mother. All we can say with certainty is that Columbanus was indeed literate and that this skill was acquired while he was living at home.

Who gave him this education? There was no shortage of monastic clergymen who could have provided the training, if it was a clergyman. Within an eight-mile arc from the eastern slopes of the Blackstairs Mountains lie four modern villages, Kildavin (about three miles north of Bunclody), Kiltealy and Killann (five and eight miles southwest of Bunclody respectively), and Kilmyshall (between Kiltealy and Bunclody, and perhaps right in the area of Columbanus' birth). These villages, like scores of others scattered across Ireland, have the prefix *Kil-*, indicating that they had their origin as a monastic settlement, or "cell." While some of these have become quite famous, such as Kilkenny and Kildare, they were not all in existence in the sixth century but were formed at some point during the first three or four centuries after St. Patrick. These local monastic villages may not have been there during Columbanus' youth, but the possibility certainly exists that he may have been instructed by a nearby monk from one of these foundations. Leinster was not a wasteland when it came to church matters. On the continent monasteries developed "inner" and "outer" schools, the former for those actually becoming monks, and the latter for young boys from secular households who were desirous of receiving a basic education. If the continental model was followed, Columbanus may have studied as a young boy at the Irish equivalent of an "outer" school. Or he may have been instructed at the family homestead by a visiting monastic tutor.

Another theory on the matter holds that Columbanus' education follows rather closely the system used on the continent. Why would a young Irish boy necessarily be educated in a continental fashion? Christianity itself, the impetus for literacy in the first place, was, after all, introduced from the continent, so why not the basic educational sequence? In later centuries the Irish would personalize their own educational system, but in the first century of Christianity in Ireland, it is plausible that Columbanus followed a continental course of study. If so, what might that course be?

A child would be instructed at his mother's knee until about the age of seven. This would be no formal education, but the basic motor skill development and attainment of a maturation level necessary to begin regular schooling. The years up to about seven were termed *infantia*. Then during the years seven to about twelve, called *pueritia*, or "boyhood," the child would receive primary instruction in reading, writing, and penmanship. From about twelve to sixteen, *adolescentia*, the student would attempt to master the complexities of Latin grammar. There developed a popular, and enduring, statement about this stage of education: "One must traverse the arid plains of Latin grammar before one reaches the delectable mountains of Latin thought." Long hours learning the proper declension and case were a distasteful prerequisite to understanding textual meaning. Finally the student was ready in the late teen years to experience the nuances of scriptural interpretation, or exegesis, as well as rhetoric, or the useful skills of developing and presenting a closely reasoned argument. This scheme would seem to fit the career of Columbanus as we know it. He appears to have spent his early years at home, instructed in the basics there until the onset of his late preteen or early teen years, then entered a monastery for additional learning, and finally, transferred to a finishing monastery for his advanced education.

However, it still requires some imaginative work to reconstruct just how a young boy like Columbanus would actually be taught basic writing skills in the mid-sixth century. Paper was prohibitively expensive, only slightly less dear was sheepskin parchment or cowhide vellum. Learning the alphabet and penmanship requires much trial and error, far too costly in terms of writing surface. Here it appears the Irish were indeed using the same techniques as on the continent. The answer was simple, as good answers frequently are. A wooden shingle slightly hollowed out to form a shallow tray was filled with melted wax. When the wax hardened, it was suitable for use as a writing tablet using a metal stylus, called a *graib*, to inscribe the words. When the lesson was done, the shingle could be held over a flame close enough to melt the wax but not so close as to light the wood. The melted wax would form a smooth liquid sheet, erasing the previous work and leaving the shingle ready for the next lesson. It was a renewable tablet allowing virtually unlimited practice to perfect the student's performance. This surpasses some earlier, more ancient, forms of learning the alphabet. In the old way, a large stone inscribed with the letters, and now called an *abecedarium* would be set up at certain points in the land much like the alphabet is posted in a primary school room today. With the wax tablets, easy transmission and practice of the alphabet became possible.

Whatever the case with the mechanisms of Columbanus' early education, both literary and practical, his career at this point would seem to be set to follow the same path as other high-born Irish nobles: leadership in the clan in secular affairs, in both war and peace. But looming over everything in Columbanus' life, and apparently playing no small role in its course, was the constant threat of death. Beginning at about the time of his birth in 543, and continuing in recurring waves for the entirety of his life, Ireland and the whole continent was visited by one of the greatest disasters in recorded history. The ever-present reality that death could harvest any and all souls at any moment had telling impact on the attitudes of Columbanus, his family and associates, and indeed society in general. It is impossible to tell the story of Columbanus' career without factoring in this disaster that so reshaped the social, political, and religious matrix from which he came and in which he lived the rest of his life.

The nature of this disaster, which is now mostly lost in the dim mists of nearly fifteen centuries of history, is problematical, but a brief survey of the scope and magnitude of the disaster is necessary to understand its pervasive effect.

The Early Medieval Plague

In the late 540s, Ireland was visited with a plague that encompassed the whole island and killed so many so quickly as to seem, in the words of a contemporary writer, "to return the world to its original silence." The plague, called in the sources the "mortalis magna," or "great death," seems to have hit Ireland in three waves initially: in 545, 550, and again in 553. This triple nightmare was the bubonic plague, so-called because a major symptom of the disease was the formation of large swellings, or buboes, in the groin, armpits, and neck. These swellings caused subcutaneous rupturing of the blood vessels in the affected areas, giving the skin there a bruised, or black-and-blue, look. This gave rise to the later common English name for the disease, the *Black Death*, as well as the French term for it, *le morte bleu*, "the Blue Death." In the sixth-century Latin sources, however, the plague has a specific name: *lues inguinaria*, "the groin disease." Today it is often called "Justinian's Plague" since it first struck during the reign of the Byzantine Emperor Justinian (r. 527–565). The contemporary French bishop and historian, Gregory of Tours (538–594), gave an excellent description of the bubonic plague: "Death came very quickly … an open sore like a snake's bite appeared in the groin or the armpit, and the man who had it soon died of its poison, breathing his last on the second or third day." In spite of its fearsome appearance, the bubonic plague was survivable, if only for the lucky few. But mostly, and certainly in popular imagination, the diagnosis of the plague seemed to mean certain death.

Within five years the plague had covered Europe. Estimates are that a third of the population perished in the opening years and by the end of the plague era nearly two centuries later, half the total population, or approximately one hundred million were thought to have died. It has been discerned that at no time during the years 540–717 was plague entirely absent from Europe. All this, of course, is hard to verify. Scholars are sometimes reduced to searching burial grounds for signs of multiple burials in a given month or season. Fortunately, the custom of Christian burial in this era favored interment at dawn, to signify the coming resurrection, with the head of the deceased buried toward the rising sun. Since the angle of sunrise is calculable, so are the burials, and so can plague visitations be reckoned.

As debatable as the mechanisms of plague origin, transmission, and mortality rates may be, they are exceeded in uncertainty by the impact of the disease itself. In a pandemic of this horrific scope, proper burial was overwhelmed by the mass casualties, fields were left untended, and livestock were free to roam ownerless. The suffocating sense of fear and panic that gripped the popular imagination can be blamed or credited for far more than it actually did. Lacking precise economic records, one can only guess at the impact of the plague on trade. The traditional view was that commerce in Western Europe was already seriously depressed by the fragmenting effects of the barbarian invasions. There seems to have been a shift away from the Mediterranean as the center of trade in favor of the more northern waters of the English Channel and North and Baltic Seas. Others have argued that the northern shift was not apparent in the immediate postinvasion period of the later 400s and early 500s. Perhaps the plague, rather than barbarian invasion, was the impetus for this reorientation. It has been noted that the plague seems to have had a more telling impact on urban areas than rural ones. Doubtless this was due to the population density in the cities, as well as the higher rat population. If so, the major cities of Europe, clustered as they were around the old Roman Mediterranean trade routes, would be decimated, leaving the smaller towns of the north in a comparatively stronger position. Economic recovery would seem to be easier in a self-sufficient rural north more so than in an urban south.

Whatever the relative impact on cities, the question remains "What was the impact of such mortality on the availability of labor?" This question always accompanies discussions of plague and is very difficult to gauge in precentralized societies. For the sixth- and seventh-century outbreak, there are no parliamentary decrees, such as those in England and France in the fourteenth-century pandemic restricting wages and prices to preplague levels. But it is assumed that the same dynamic was at work in the age of Justinian's Plague. That dynamic is based on the fact that the plague was no respecter of persons, killing skilled and unskilled laborers alike. Therefore crafted goods rose in price sharply, since skilled craftsmen cannot be replaced quickly, creating economic distress for the upper classes who are the market for these same crafted goods. This would have impact on Columbanus' family who, while not known to be of the very highest rank, were certainly above the norm in their material goods. Additionally, common laborers were increasingly scarce in this age of high mortality, giving even unskilled workers a bit more leverage in wage matters. How this actually played out is lost in the silence of unrecorded history, but some believe it may have been the impetus, or at least a major one, in the diminishing of slavery and its eventual replacement with the status of serfdom. It all speaks to the pervasive dislocation of the economy and its connected social structure.

The economic argument for a shift of power from urban south to rural north is almost inseparable from the political theory as well. The postinvasion world was very much an agrarian one featuring the earliest versions of what would be the medieval manorial system. Cities were shrunken affairs; reduced to only a small defensible core. Luxury structures such as baths and arenas were either abandoned or dismantled to create a smaller, more defensible city perimeter. The cities still held the administrative offices of the church, usually the bishop and his *domus*, or household, but were commercially as well as militarily no longer as important. The hunting lodges of barbarian kings, located in the dense forests, were now the seats of power rather than an administrative city capital. This dovetailed nicely with the barbarian view of the personalization of government: Wherever the king was, that was the "king's peace." The person of the king rather than a capital city was the key element in political power.

Once again, the obvious dislocation of the old systems and their apparent reconfiguration leaves much room for expansive theories. Some see the ultimate collapse of Justinian's reconquest of the old, lost provinces of the Roman Empire as caused by the plague sapping Byzantine power. Even the rise of Islam, in the 630s, is viewed as possible only because a plague-weakened Byzantium had little or nothing left after defeating the Persians in 628. The ascendancy of the rural north, a by-product of the plague, is used to explain the rise of the Frankish kingdom in Gaul, and the emergence of the Lombards in northern Italy; both developments will figure in a major way in Columbanus' later career.

Back in Ireland, which had no real urban centers that might be emptied by plague, the situation was somewhat different. Here the plague would cut a similar swath through all levels of society. Some have argued that the eastern seaboard, extending between the present locations of Dublin and Cork, was more trade oriented than the rest of the island and thus harder hit by the plague. This, it is said, opened the door for the emergence of a heretofore obscure family from the more rural northwest: the Uí Neill. There seems to be evidence to support a changing of the guard across the island. The Uí Neill would not complete their ascendancy until the eleventh century, but other, local chieftains and their families would come from the shadows to command a portion of Ireland. Such were the Uí Duncaigne rulers of Leinster, Columbanus' homeland. They ruled from the sixth century to the ninth century, when the massive disruption of the Viking invasions reshuffled power in Ireland generally.

But for our purposes, the most intangible factors are the key ones. In an era that saw the plague threaten to wipe out mankind, the economy morph into new and uncertain structures, the political situation change as rapidly and thoroughly as a kaleidoscope, and, to add to the swirling change, a new religion just putting down roots in the land, the whole of society must have seemed in chaos. Perhaps the biggest change, then, might be that of attitude. It would be difficult to see the world in the same way when all around you is becoming unrecognizable. It is, therefore, not surprising that an old Irish saying had its birth in this volatile age, "There are three periods in which the world is worthless: the time of plague, the time of a general war, and the dissolution of express contracts." The world did indeed seem worthless to those caught up in this maelstrom. If another old saying, not of Irish provenance, is true that "fear concentrates the mind wonderfully," then it might also be true that fear of imminent death reorders priorities dramatically.

This imminent death, as well as the very capriciousness of death encapsulated in the puzzle of why one would die yet another survive, can elicit wildly differing responses. Some, thinking today is their last day, may become deeply religious, while others, equally convinced that the end is quite near, may become all the more reckless and wanton. Even so some Christians would not allow the probability of near death to modify their questionable behavior significantly. Such was the supposedly Christian Irish king of the late 590s, who, having vanquished a key opponent in a bloody battle, took his adversary's head back home as a trophy. This was an old pagan Celtic custom so prevalent that some scholars have spoken of a "cult of the severed head." These grisly mementoes would be displayed with pride in the victor's house and apparently satisfied some primal need for sympathetic magic. In that view "like produces like," so that if one fought and defeated a particularly brave foe, the taking of his head would give you that bravery as well. The "Christian" king in question was in for a shock, however, as when he tied the long hair of the severed head to his saddle horn and began the bumpy ride back home, the teeth from the open mouth cut his exposed thigh. The king's wound became infected and he died, giving the beheaded rival the ultimate revenge.

But those who were truly serious about their faith, or even those who saw in the great mortality the punishing hand of an angry God, were given to amend their pagan ways and forsake this world for an eternal one. The fact that all that seemed certain about the temporal world was in disarray only underscored the message that renouncing this world in favor of the other was the only sensible thing to do. The renunciation of the present world would, in effect, take the sting out of death. One would not fear losing what one had already forsaken. This became an increasingly common attitude, not only in Ireland, but in the rest of Christian Europe as well. At the little Anglo-Saxon settlement of Barking, site of a convent, the plague began to kill the sisters off in relentless fashion. Rather than worry or panic over the coming annihilation, the abbess simply went from nun to nun and asked them to pick out their own burial spots. The French social historian Philippe Ariès made this supernaturally calm acceptance of death a major feature in his history of death customs in Europe. He called it "tame death," and lamented the fact that modern people lacked this ancient view that death was a natural, and inevitable, part of the life cycle. Whether natural or not, or, more probably only confined to the monastic culture, the rejection of the world and its accompanying lack of fear concerning death, was certainly heightened by the recurring visitations of the plague.

If an Irishman were to decide to renounce this world in favor of another, where might he go to accomplish this? The most obvious places were the monasteries and convents of the age. One might expect them to feel the loss of population as much as the rest of society, and they did, but they seem to have grown disproportionately in numbers during this period as waves of people fled the tumult seeking refuge. In fact, the monasteries were largely modeled after the social structure of early Ireland. So even as they fled society, the monks would enter an alternative one that was in some ways strangely familiar. The monastery was like the dun, complete with protective wall and the restrictions against strangers having access to the interior where only the monastic family, like the fine, could go. The Irish word for family eventually came to be *muinter*, a corruption of the word *monastery*. When a man or woman forsook the present social world, he or she could therefore become a member of a world shaped in familiar fashion like the old, but based on eternal values. It was different yet the same, the challenge of the new, yet with the comfort of recognizable organization.

One might expect the monasteries to become larger, despite the mortality, during the plague era. But that would be a development that would occur generally after the plague had subsided. What happened was a proliferation of the number of monasteries, not a massive growth in size. An excellent example is that of St. Finnian's monastery at Clonard on the lovely River Boyne in east central Ireland. Finnian, sometimes called "Vinnian" in the sources, was a Leinsterman like Columbanus, although of some two generations earlier. He apparently studied in Wales under St. Cadoc and was close to Gildas, who would write about the Anglo-Saxon invasions of Britain, thereby giving rise to the Arthurian legend. About the year 520, Finnian founded his major monastery at *Cluain Erard* (Clonard, or "high meadow"), and it soon became the cradle of many of the most famous saints in Ireland. When the first wave of the plague hit, about 548, the elderly Finnian was an early victim. A monastery well established for nearly thirty years, Clonard should have simply selected a new abbot and continued as before. But in the early generations of Irish monasticism, much like the first universities of Europe some seven centuries later, the monastery itself was not the draw for new members, but the famous man. In this era, sainthood was conferred by popular acclaim—the structured church process of today was not in force. So when Finnian died, for a time his foundation of Clonard ceased to exist. The students scattered throughout Ireland and founded their own monasteries based in varying degrees on Finnian's model. The most famous pupils, called in church lore "the Twelve Apostles of Ireland," were like dandelion seeds blown by the wind spreading monasticism wherever they lighted. In a way the plague dispersed rather than concentrated the monastic presence and the eager young converts willing to forsake the world and their own families more than replenished the numbers lost due to Justinian's Plague. In a strange symbiotic way, monasticism became as widespread throughout the island as the plague itself.

But what does the spread of monasticism have to do with Columbanus? Given the line of development of his life up to his teen years, it might have had nothing to do with him. As it turned out, it had everything to do with what he became. The young Columbanus—talented, blond, muscular, and well connected—would come of age in a world that offered a popular spiritual alternative to the chaos all around. But how did this fine lad become attuned to the monastic world of ascetic self-denial? There would be a personal crisis that would ignite, or perhaps direct, an inclination that may have been lying dormant deep within his heart.

3

The Call

The story of Columbanus' call to his life's work as a monk, monastic founder, missionary, and, by the force of his personality and ideas, contributor to Western Civilization, is left remarkably free of details by his biographer Jonas of Bobbio. The young Columbanus, just coming into manhood, is described as "having a fine figure." His good looks attracted the advances of young women around him, and he became troubled about this. Seeking an answer to his uneasiness, he sought out a female Christian hermit whose solitary abode was nearby. She advised him to flee temptations like these and enter a monastery. The most momentous decision of his life is described in terms just this maddeningly sparse.

It might be sparse, but not unusual for the era. One of the features of the first centuries after the fall of Rome is an emphasis on deeds at the expense of intention. The "what" of an action is described, but not the "why." Consequently, great turning points are recorded without a hint of what prompted the decisions. A classic example is that of the father of Western monasticism, Benedict of Nursia (480–543), and his rejection of Eastern monasticism in favor of a new system. His new approach, called *Benedictine monasticism* in his honor, would be based on the premise that it is much better to consecrate the body to service than to destroy it with self-mortification. This shift in thinking sanctified labor as embodied in Benedict's motto, *Laborare est Orare* ("to work is to pray"), and has been widely credited with forming the basis of Western ideas of progress. Benedict's decision to leave one style of monastic life and create another is therefore one of the most significant changes of heart in history. But, as with Columbanus, we know nothing of what prompted this radical step nor of the inner workings of Benedict's mind as he came to this conclusion.

Despite the unadorned prose and lack of a hint as to motivation, we might surmise that something was already at work in Columbanus' heart even before he received his monastic call. What was it, for example, that made him seek a spiritual answer when tempted by the charms of young women? Accounts of his life leave this unexamined for good reason: We simply cannot know. But something might have already existed in his soul that led to this response. When one is shaken, what is inside spills out. Why didn't Columbanus simply succumb to the allure of the women? Why would he seek counsel by visiting, of all things, a holy *woman* hermit? Did he suffer from an excess of sincerity? Was he unable to take Christian teachings on proper sexual behavior with a wink and a nod? The unyielding conviction manifested in his later career would seem to demonstrate this in full. We do know that Columbanus was instructed in the first level of his education in the Christian scriptures and quite possibly in some of the theological works of the Church fathers as well. Augustine's *De Doctrina Christiana* was popular in Ireland from an early date. As a teenager Columbanus probably had several years of tutoring in the rudiments of the Christian faith.

But that too begs the question: Why would Christian teachings encourage a young man to flee from contact with the opposite sex? But flee he certainly did. Jonas relates that the advice Columbanus received was directly to that point. He quoted the Roman writer Livy that "no one is rendered so sacred by religion, no one so guarded, that lust is unable to prevail against him." The comely maidens were described as "deadly weapons," and Jonas used warlike imagery to depict Columbanus' resistance to their advances. The anchoress told him to take the shield and the two-edged sword of the Gospel to fight off the temptations before him. Jonas quoted the holy woman, using the common literary device of placing the desired point into a fictitious conversation, as asking the earnest young man if he thought he could "associate with the female sex without sin?" She rained biblical examples ranging from Adam and Eve to Samson and Delilah to David and Bathsheba on the hapless Columbanus to drive the point home. Why was there such evident hostility to sex, which, after all, was instituted by God Himself?

Here once again, history is both the captor and the captive of its time. The prevalent view in Christian teaching during the rapid spread of the faith in the fourth and fifth centuries was to purify sexual practices. Monogamy, fidelity in marriage, and chastity before marriage were emphasized. One of the early complaints by the Roman world was that Christians were forbidding slave owners from having sex with their slave girls, an unheard of imposition. But from this drive to conform sexual practices to Christian principles, the movement grew to view sex in general as to be avoided by those truly spiritually serious. St. Augustine, when asked by one of the parishioners in his diocese in North Africa what was the main point of origin for sin, answered *Ecce unde* ("Look below"), a clear reference to the genital area. Another influential voice, St. Jerome (347–419), railed against marriage, arguing that lifelong virginity was the preferable state for a real Christian. He compared virginity to wheat, marriage to barley, and fornication to cattle dung. His concluding advice was that "to prevent a person pressed by hunger from eating cow dung, I may allow him to eat barley." These famous voices were just a few of the multitudes preaching that the blandishments of the opposite sex were to be avoided if at all possible.

Of course moral lapses were not the sole property of the Irish in the sixth century. The evidence from across Europe seems to indicate that, despite the Church's increasingly stringent stand against sexual promiscuity, the general standard of behavior was somewhat loose. Frankish kings, for example, regularly married multiple partners with the proviso that whichever consort could produce the first son, and therefore the next king, would be recognized as the queen. Even the clergy was far from the celibate order of later centuries. Married priests were so common that their wives even had a special term in the sources: *presbyterissa*, the feminine version of *presbyter*, or priest. It is true that some of these women so designated were the wives of men who, after marriage, became priests and from that point on treated their wives as sisters rather than true spouses. But most of the time the term signified a full marriage relationship, sex and all. The result was that there was a possibility of a hereditary priesthood as sons could succeed fathers. This was one of the practices that the push for clerical celibacy hoped to avoid: the sense of entitlement and ownership leading to corruption within the priesthood. Years later a celibate priesthood would win out, but in the sixth and seventh centuries the issue was still in doubt, despite the influential arguments on its behalf.

The Monastic Answer

There was, however, one segment of the Church for which there could be no doubt about celibacy: monasticism. The earliest forms of monasticism originated in the red land desert beyond the Nile Valley of Egypt and the forbidding Syrian wilderness. The goal was mortification of the flesh and it is useful to note that the root of that word is the Latin for death, *mors*. These Eastern monks became so zealous in their attempts to destroy the flesh in order that the soul would be free to commune with God that they committed infamous excesses. They deprived themselves of food, water, sleep, all forms of bodily comfort, and contact with the opposite sex as a means of refining their holiness. It has been suggested that they were, in effect, "monastic athletes" who were constantly trying to break their own personal record for self-mortification. But this was not the view in Europe or in Columbanus' Ireland.

Some have noted that Irish monasticism of the sixth and seventh centuries was closer to the Egyptian model than to later Western ones. To a certain degree this is correct. The actual monastic settlements of the early days in Ireland did resemble the first monastic communities in the eastern Mediterranean. And the Irish did practice a robust form of self-denial: one thing that appealed to the intense Columbanus. But the extreme practices that pepper the accounts of Eastern monasticism seem to be very rare in the West of Columbanus' day. The model there was not so much an "athlete" always striving to outdo himself in mortification as it was the "soldier" who did his duty fully but stayed within the expected "orders of the day." St. Martin of Tours (316?–397), the archetypal soldier-saint of Late Antiquity, may have set the tone for this. He likened the Christian communities to military camps and suggested that a good monk would follow orders. This seems to be the earliest manifestation of the *Milites Christi*, "soldiers of Christ," concept that would become a staple of Medieval Christendom.

But this difference between Eastern and Western practice should not mislead us into thinking that there was a lessening of monastic prohibition against consorting with the opposite sex. The accepted ideal was complete celibacy, even if the actual behavior often failed to achieve that. It seems Columbanus, sincere and fervent in his religion as he was, would seek to meet the standard rather than circumvent it. Years later he would write in a poem titled *De Mundi Transitu*, "On the Passage of the World," these words of advice: "Beware my little son, the forms of women, through whom death enters, no light destruction." Perhaps he, like so many others have done in history, allowed a personal crisis to become a general principle.

Advice from an Anchoress

So it was that the troubled young man sought out a holy anchoress, thought to be Croine Beag, the sister of a local king named Ainmire, who had her solitary abode in the vicinity of Carlow, very near Columbanus' dun. An anchoress, the feminine version of anchorite, was one who practiced *anachoresis*, or the shunning of society by "going up country." In effect an anchorite was a hermit who voluntarily withdrew from all social contact to better concentrate on the worship of God and the mortification of the flesh. We might think this odd today, but in Columbanus' time these were the stars of popular piety. So much was this the case that a steady stream of petitioners and would-be emulators came to these recluses, spoiling their solitude with questions and unwanted company. An excellent example of this occurred just a few miles to the northeast of Columbanus' home where St. Kevin, desiring to be alone, set up camp in a small cave in the Wicklow Mountains overlooking a glen between two beautiful freshwater lakes. The word soon got out that a holy man was living up in the hills, and so many imitators came to gather round him that he was unable to drive them off. Eventually giving up, Kevin organized the group into a monastic community that became known as Glendalough, or "the glen between the lakes." This was a common scenario, not only in Ireland but throughout the monastic world. It was so common that some scholars of the monastic movement consider eremitic monasticism, the solitary "hermit" type, to be the first necessary step toward cenobitic, or group, monasticism. But some anchorites were successful in remaining alone, and even occasionally available as counselors. Such was the anchoress we believe to be Croine Beag.

Thus far accounts of Columbanus' decisive turning point make a critical assumption: that he was already drawn to monastic life. It would seem to fit the situation. Columbanus could have taken the anchoress' advice against promiscuity as a way to keep himself chaste until marriage. In that scenario he would have taken his place in regular Irish society as a clan leader; married a well-connected bride; and lived a full, although for our purposes, anonymous life. It seems that he was looking for more than fidelity but rather for monastic commitment. Either the anchoress was a fabulously persuasive advocate, or

Columbanus was an easy sell on the idea. He willingly and quickly took her words to heart. But even then, the question arises "Why monasticism?" Could not Columbanus have become a priest rather than one who sought solitude—*monachism*, the root word of monasticism, means "solitude." Once again a plausible explanation is that he wanted the most intense and fully committed lifestyle available. There must have been a precondition favoring this already in his heart. Thus, it was that the young man came away from this encounter convinced to enter a monastery.

Telling His Mother

The surety of his decision put him in a delicate position. As a dutiful son who knew full well the scriptural admonition to "honor your father and mother," Columbanus may have felt some inner conflict about monasticism's impact on his family. Centuries later, the Irish monasteries would maintain family ties in their structure. Certain leading families would control the position of abbot, while kinsmen would live in what amounted to monastic towns around the edge of the monastery proper. But in the first stage of monasticism in Ireland, entering a monastery was much like death. The monk was so removed from family, and so permanently, that it might as well be as if he were dead. Was it disobedience to forsake family? In our contemporary society, enamored of personal choice, we might say that he was a rebel resisting society's expectations. But there is another possible explanation that seems to fit Columbanus' personality. He might have been obeying rather than rebelling, but obeying what he saw as a higher authority than even his family: the call of God. But whether or not that was his view, there was still the matter of actually making the break with his kin and, in particular, his mother.

That confrontation became one of the most heart-wrenching and dramatic moments in Columbanus' career. Even the unadorned description of Jonas' biography cannot mask the intensity. We don't know how Columbanus raised the issue with his mother. Given the brusque approach he employed throughout his career with kings, queens, bishops, and even popes, one wonders if he did not simply come into his home and blurt out his fateful decision. Whether done diplomatically or not, the news appears to have been devastating. His mother reacted hysterically, begging him to change his mind and even clinging to his leg in a vain attempt to stop his leaving. The distraught woman finally threw herself across the threshold to their home forcing Columbanus to break with his loving family both physically and emotionally by stepping over her body to depart. The resolute young saint was made to declare, using the words of Jesus, "Haven't you heard that whoever loves father and mother more than me is not worthy of me?" With that, he strode purposefully out the door and toward an uncertain future.

The whole scene bears a strong resemblance to a passage in St. Jerome's writings in which he advised a young man contemplating entry into the monastic life just like Columbanus. The testy old saint recounted that he told the young man, "Depart, though your mother tear her hair and rend her garments, though your father lie flat upon the threshold of his house to stay your going, trample forth over him." With that, Jerome concluded, "Your only love and duty in this business is to be cruel." One can approach this in three ways. Perhaps Jonas of Bobbio crafted his account of Columbanus' break with his mother using Jerome as a model. Maybe Columbanus himself had read Jerome, a definite possibility in Ireland, and reenacted the necessary break based on what he had read. Or it could be that neither Columbanus nor Jonas knew of Jerome's description. It might have been a mere coincidence that the two accounts resemble each other so closely. This is a fairly frequent dilemma when dealing with Late Antique and Early Medieval sources, particularly when the author is re-creating a scene or conversation from the past.

Whether contrived, copied, or legitimate, Columbanus' break with his mother and family calls another question to mind. While it is certainly understandable that his mother was distraught, some parents might have weathered this kind of shock a bit more readily. Why was she so terribly devastated? Columbanus' father is conspicuously absent from the story. Some have surmised that he may have been a victim of the plague, perhaps making Columbanus' mother overly protective of her son. No other brothers or sisters are mentioned in the sources. Perhaps they never existed, or were plague victims themselves. If so, his mother would be left unprotected when her only son opted to leave the home and the duties of the fine for a distant monastery. The charm of the fine, that your family is always there to protect and succor you, weakens in direct proportion to the decrease in fine members. The same dynamic was at work on the continent, and explains why the early Germanic law codes sought to avoid and mediate feuds. The end result of a feud is the extinguishing of one family and the possible reduction of the other to the point of near defenselessness. Anyone left without kindred was one left without protection.

But it is highly unlikely that Columbanus' mother would be left alone at the dun. Other extended family would be there. She would, however, be without a direct shield of support as a widow without a surviving child to take her side. Years later in medieval France, a woman in this predicament was labeled as *descouverte*, or "discovered," meaning that she was left vulnerable to the predatory plans of the enemies of her late husband or children. Even dwelling among friendly members of her clan, her position would be in perilous decline. Perhaps Columbanus' mother was not only emotionally devastated by his departure but also was deprived socially.

Heeding the Call

Nevertheless, Columbanus was resolute in his decision. After all, a call only becomes a vocation if it is heeded; otherwise it is no more than a passing feeling. But the heeding of the call opened up an even more pressing question than it answered. Where would this potential monk enter a monastery? In the early years of Irish monasticism, the monks did not go to a famous monastery so much as they went to study under a famous monk. And in Columbanus' case, his choice of monastery coincided with the plague-induced fanning out of famous, well-trained monks founding new monastic communities.

Columbanus' selection, however, has puzzled historians ever since and given rise to multiple theories. The headstrong young Columbanus opted to journey far afield, to the northwestern portion of Ireland and the waters of Lower Lough Erne. This had become an active center of monasticism in Ireland. When St. Finnian of Clonard had died of the plague in 548, and his disciples scattered to start their own foundations, no less than four of them went to small islands in the Lough Erne area. It was to Sinell's community, located on the island called *Cluain Inish*, or "meadow isle," later to morph into Cleenish, that Columbanus set his course. It would be a trip of well over 150 miles using various streams and tracks in what was certainly no mean feat of travel in this age.

Given that there were other, closer monasteries, some perhaps in the near vicinity to Columbanus' dun, the question of "Why this monastery?" begs an answer. Plausible theories circulate around two points. First, Cleenish would offer one of the most highly respected versions of monastic life in Ireland. Sinell's pedigree, coming as he did from the tutelage of the famed St. Finnian, was impeccable. That tradition alone would be capable of drawing a young man from so far away, especially if he were fervent to have the best that monasticism could offer. Second, there appears to have been a territorial kinship between Columbanus and the Cleenish tradition, if not a direct family connection. St. Finnian, the spiritual ancestor of the community, is believed to have been born at Myshall, later to be called Kilmyshall, literally in the backyard of Columbanus' dun. Further, Sinell is thought to have been a Leinsterman as well, perhaps with clan ties to Columbanus. So the double attraction of fame and kinship drew the young man northwest regardless of the perils and difficulties of the journey.

And difficulties there would be. Travel was a life-threatening experience in a land mostly wilderness with predatory animals, bandits, and treacherous natural hazards. It was, for example, common practice for a traveler to carry a long pole when crossing one of the many bogs in Ireland. This was necessary to test the path; for that which appeared to be solid land was often a morass in disguise. The long pole could sound out the worthiness of the footpath, preventing one from sinking in something like quicksand.

There were few acceptable thoroughfares for long-distance travel in sixth-century Ireland. Aside from the rivers and streams, there were a handful of *sligeda*, or "cuttings," roads fashioned out of the gravel ridges that occasionally cut through the island. But there were no sligeda in Columbanus' region, probably forcing him to use the waterways as his principal transportation.

Whatever route he took, whether it was by boat or foot, it was an arduous and dangerous journey. Apparently the teenage Columbanus made the trek alone, no doubt traveling only in the daylight to avoid the pitfalls of wild animals and natural obstacles that could be so lethal. Even during the day, pewter skies, wind-swept rain, and the necessity of finding food and potable water made the trip quite a challenge. A saving grace was no doubt the old Irish custom of hospitality, giving a wayfarer such as our young would-be monk a decent chance at shelter and a meal as he went from dun to dun. Oddly, as difficult as the journey may have been, it was perhaps better in material comfort than the life of renunciation that Columbanus was voluntarily embracing. The young Columbanus was indeed a highly motivated recruit for Sinell's school. That motivation was to be an abiding characteristic of the man for his entire career. It would provide a sort of glow, or radiance, that would set him apart and inform his every action. It would also irradiate every place and peoples he encountered.

Into the Monasteries

When Columbanus arrived at the watery fastness of Sinell's monastery at Cleenish, he was entering a lifestyle that would be his until his death nearly sixty years later. It would also be the public phase of his life, when he emerged upon the stage of European history out of the relative obscurity of the monastic world. Would he shine forth, in the words of his birthdream, with a radiance that would light entire nations? Radiance and light was decidedly not what he found at Cleenish. The windswept wetness on the tiny island was in contrast to his home snug against the protective eminence of the Blackstairs Mountains. The people of the Lough Erne area, where Cleenish is located, have a saying about the seasonal weather there: "In the summer Lough Erne is in County Fermanagh, in the winter County Fermanagh is in Lough Erne." Driving rain and flooding made the discipline at Cleenish all the more telling.

But it was not the lure of fame that brought Columbanus to Sinell and Cleenish in the first place. While it is true that, unlike today when saints are made according to a precise and demanding formula, according to contemporary Irish custom, all those who devoted themselves exclusively to the religious life were called *saints*. Even though we know several hundred of these saints' names, the reality was that when one went into a monastery, generally one became anonymous. *Famous monks* are so few, given that the several hundred we know span many centuries, that the term is almost an oxymoron. Anyone predicting Columbanus' future as he journeyed to Cleenish would say, "That's the last we will hear of him." The triple monastic vow of poverty, chastity, and obedience was not calculated to create celebrity. Even Sinell himself was famous against his will. All the sources call him a hermit, which makes no sense when the legions of young monks who studied at Cleenish are tallied up. But this is probably yet another version of the common monastic development where a religious hermit eventually attracts so many unwanted disciples that he relents and forms them into a monastery. Perhaps Sinell, feeling the loss of his master Finnian of Clonard, went west to Cleenish to be alone, only to find himself surrounded by pupils begging for instruction and leadership. The monastic community sometimes just happened without extensive planning.

Once the community existed, however, it rapidly developed a type of infrastructure and a corresponding set of customs. The first order of business, especially in a harsh environment such as that of Cleenish, would be establishing some sort of shelter. Irish monks built, usually with their own hands, wattle and daub huts called *boothies*. Later, in areas with plentiful rocks, the boothies could be of stacked stone. But generally they were of the same homemade construction as that of the typical peasant hut. In fact everything about the monks and their monastery was at the level of the peasant rather than the noble, in spite of the upper-class family ties of many of the monks. It would have been difficult to renounce the world in comfort. So the monks made their own clothes and at first they must have been a ragtag looking lot. Later a rather standard garb would emerge of white woolen robes, a girdle, cloak, and hood being the preferred dress. Simple sandals were the common footwear.

These young men, whether highborn or not, were expected to work daily, which symbolized their changed life. In early Ireland, work was considered something that only the lower classes did. A man falling on hard times could sell himself into slavery for a period equivalent to his debt, a system much like that found in ancient Athens before the great lawgiver Solon abolished debt slavery for citizens. The similarities in the systems brought about a similar by-product: the association of manual labor with low social status. So when monks set about their daily fieldwork, they were making a hugely symbolic statement about their renunciation of the privileges of the world. But the symbolism extended beyond labor and dress. While these young men might have been adept at cattle ranching, hunting, and trapping game, they normally would have left the cooking to the women of the dun. Yet the monks at the monastery would eat vegetables, herbs, and bread in one meal a day, usually at about three in the afternoon. Owing to their lack of cooking experience, the denial of the flesh through meager rations was no doubt reinforced by the absence of culinary skills among the brothers.

Once again the diet matched the clothes, huts, and workload: all indicating that the monks were voluntarily taking the lowest rung on the social ladder. Years later, Columbanus would preach a sermon on this attitude of self-denial and conclude, "The man for whom little is not enough will not benefit from more." It has been said, eloquently, of these monks that they were "acquiring the riches of absolute poverty." It would seem their lifestyle was calculated to accomplish just that.

The Work of Worship

But Cleenish was not just a grouping of huts containing monks who went about their separate business. A community must have a common point of collection and ritual. So it was that early on the monasteries built churches for worship, followed soon by a dual-purpose library and classroom structure. The basic purpose of the monastery was to worship God, not only in self-denial or even in field labor, but also in the act of group worship and, most importantly, in an Ireland afire with a zeal for learning, in education as well. Once again the early churches, libraries, and even cafeterias (in later monastic history called *refectories*), were made of wood and mud. Only later, primarily from the early tenth century on, would stone structures emerge such as the tiny, quaint churches and the photogenic round stone bell towers, or *cloicteach*, used to store valuables, call the monks to prayer, and keep a sharp eye out for would-be attackers. Lacking these later architectural refinements, in Columbanus' day Cleenish might well have resembled an encampment more than a settled community. But this "encampment" was a beehive of educational activity. The Irish had revered a god of knowledge, Ogmios, and once they became Christian they believed wholeheartedly in the power of education. If there was one thing that marked monasteries such as Cleenish, it was a deep love of learning. While the monks were schooled in the works of classical antiquity, the extent of which remains a point of scholarly debate, their main objective was the study of the scriptures, the *lectio divina*, or "divine readings." Thus, the library was a focal point for the monastery. But we should not envision it as a modern library, with rows of shelved books. The building was quite small, the study being done mostly outdoors. Tales of Irish saints sitting in the woods or tall grass while studying their readings and being aided by friendly animals such as foxes, birds, and squirrels are common in the literature. The library held the scrolls—bound books with pages were a later invention—in leather book satchels, which were then hung on pegs in the wall.

The monks didn't just do a readings course, however. The master of the school would quiz them on their subjects in order to evaluate their progress. According to Jonas, Sinell frequently subjected young Columbanus to a series of questions designed to test not only his grasp of information but also his ability to evaluate and apply that material. It sounds very much like the ancient Socratic method, and we know it was much in vogue in sixth-century Europe. Writers even used a fictitious version of this question-answer-discussion style to explain their positions on matters, particularly theology. Pope Gregory the Great (r. 590–604), whose career would intersect with Columbanus' years later, also employed this style in many of his famous written dialogues. In later Irish monasteries there was a hierarchy for the instructors, the highest of whom was the *fer leighann*, or master teacher. In the early days, such as those at Columbanus' Cleenish, the instruction was carried out by the abbot himself. So it was Sinell, the great teacher who studied under the legendary St. Finnian of Clonard, who trained Columbanus.

Either the training was exceptional, or Columbanus was already quite learned, for the results were impressive, and rapid. He appears to have been at Cleenish only two or three years; three being the best guess since that later became the standard period of the novitiate, or trial term for a would-be monk. Within this time Columbanus is said to have written poems and a commentary on the Psalms, which is now lost. It is noteworthy that Columbanus—learned as he was becoming in the study of classical authors, Horace and Virgil for example—did not write a work on them, but on scripture. In keeping with the Irish monastic tradition, divine readings were the main object of study. Classical literature could polish and refine style, but only as an aid, not the principal topic.

This lost commentary on the Psalms, which Columbanus produced when he was perhaps less than twenty years old, has become the source of much speculation. Later references to it indicate that it was a work of the first rank, quite a precocious accomplishment for one so young. Further, it appears to have been based on an earlier Latin version by Julian of Eclanum that was itself based on an even earlier work by Theodore of Mopsuestia. Why should this matter? As it turns out this Theodore of Mopsuestia was of questionable doctrinal orthodoxy and his writings were presently at the center of a huge theological debate that would be called *The Three Chapters Controversy*. Columbanus, apparently ignorant of the brewing theological storm, is thought to have absorbed something of the point of view of Theodore as he developed his own work. Years later as he finished his career in Lombardy in northern Italy, he would be challenged as a heretic because of his familiarity with Theodore's writings. His early exposure to Theodore opened him to later danger. This was not uncommon in the first five or six centuries of the Christian era. Some who accepted the correct teachings of the day were later astonished to find their beliefs classified as an out-of-fashion and sometimes dangerous heresy only a few years later. A famous example was the missionary to the Goths, Ulfilas (311–383), who became an Arian Christian when such was considered orthodox, and took that version of the faith to the Goths, who then entered the Roman Empire as not only invaders but heretics to boot. Even though Columbanus' youthful Three Chapters affiliation would come back to haunt him later in life, at this time in the early 560s, it helped the young Columbanus set himself apart as a student of real distinction.

We must not, however, focus too much on the educational side of monasteries such as Cleenish at the expense of the importance of worship. Worship was, after all, the very reason for the education given there. Life was to be completely consecrated to God, as the old hymn of St. Patrick illustrated. This song, supposedly composed on the spur of the moment as Patrick led his fellow priests to meet the pagan high king Leary at the sacred Hill of Tara, was popular in the monasteries of Ireland. It was called by various names. One, "The Deer's Cry," signified that as Patrick and his men walked toward Leary, who planned to kill them, they supernaturally appeared as deer in his sight. Needless to say, this befuddled the fierce king so greatly that he didn't kill the priests. Another common name for the hymn was "The Lorica," recalling the Roman breastplate with fish-scale mail to protect the soldier in battle. The hymn that safeguarded Patrick and his followers was like a musical breastplate, hence the name. We cannot be sure that it was chanted at Cleenish; many scholars believe that there was a break in the sixth-century Irish church between Patrick's tradition, organized on the Episcopal model popular on the continent, and the emerging monasteries that wished to organize the church with abbots as the leaders. However that may or may not be, Patrick's hymn was sung across the land in later centuries and, for our purposes, sums up the attitude of the early monks at monasteries such as Cleenish: that all life was to be consecrated to God and placed under his protection. "The Lorica" is quite lengthy, but in it the singer commits to "God's might to direct me, God's power to protect me, God's wisdom for learning, God's eye for discerning, God's ear for my hearing, God's word for my clearing." God is also invoked against "snares of the Devil," and against both "vice's temptation, and wrong inclination." All in all it sounds like the mission statement for the typical Irish monastery and closes with the prayer that, "Christ be with me, Christ beneath me, Christ within me, Christ behind me, Christ be o'er me, Christ before me." These men had, despite their all too human lapses, a single-minded devotion. Columbanus certainly shared in this worldview.

If "The Lorica" is an accurate guide to the intentions and motivations of these early Irish monks, we may be correct in assuming that all their labors were consecrated to God. The making of shelter and clothing, tending crops, milking cows, and the daily studies were considered a form of worship very similar to the beliefs of the continental Benedictine monks. This similarity of perspective may go far in explaining the later blending of these two styles under Columbanus' leadership in Gaul and Italy.

While all endeavors can be cast as worship, the purest form was the actual gathering together of the monks to observe what was called the *Celebration of the Divine Praises*, or corporate worship. Eight times during the twenty-four-hour day the monks would gather to sing the Psalms, a system that would survive in Western monasticism long after the Celtic form of monasticism would vanish. All the monks would rise at midnight for prayer, then again at dawn to begin the day's labor, and retire at sundown. The number of Psalms to be sung was adjusted to fit the "succession of the seasons" as Columbanus would later write. With longer nights in the winter, and longer days in the summer, the balance of daytime Psalms and nighttime Psalms would be adjusted accordingly. As Columbanus would explain it years later, "It is fitting that it be longer in the long nights and shorter in the short ones." All adjustments in quantity aside, the end result was that the Irish monastery focused heavily on worship, prayer, and the repetition of Scripture. What Columbanus learned there became the ingrained model for his own later foundations that would faithfully transport this system to the continent where it would form a contributory stream in the growing flow of Western monasticism as a whole.

But Columbanus' personality, so much on display in his long career on the continent, was not the personality of a perfectly controlled, almost inhuman saint. He frequently lost his temper, misspoke, and could hold a grudge. Yet the ideal of the monastery was just that, an ideal. Constant discipline and supervision was needed to keep the men in accordance with this lofty objective. One way this was done was by what seems a very modern technique: interpersonal accountability. Any difficult undertaking tempts the individual to ease up or skip the tougher parts of the task, yet when one has a partner to point out the need for perseverance, success is far more possible. The Irish monasteries had just such a structure. Called *anamchara*, or "soul-friend," it was the pairing up of the monks in order that they might encourage and monitor each other in this exceptional pursuit of an almost impossible ideal. On a practical level, it suited the housing situation too. The little boothies, or huts, were better inhabited by two monks, much like a college dormitory room. It is not clear if roommates were always soul-friends, or if they were assigned or chose soul-friends from other members of the monastery. Each approach had its strengths. Roommates might agree to cover for one another's laxity, while a nonroommate anamchara might not know whether or not his accountability partner was actually keeping monastic rules. But with the soul-friend structure in place, the monks were more likely to live the monastic lifestyle on a consistent basis. We don't know whether Columbanus had a soul-friend at Cleenish, and if he did, that individual's name. We may surmise, however, that he participated fully and successfully in the common life of Sinell's monastic community.

Moving On

The puzzling thing about Columbanus' stay at Cleenish is not his brilliance— his later career confirms that—but the brevity of his time there. Why did he feel compelled to leave after no more than three years? A standard interpretation is to note that young Irish monks had a tendency to migrate from monastery to monastery before settling down. Once again, the draw of a particular monastery was the famous teacher-saint rather than the institution itself. St. Columba of Iona, for example, went to at least three monastic centers for schooling and perhaps a fourth before studying under Finnian of Moville, and then on to Finnian of Clonard's famous monastery. This was not unusual and seems to give sufficient cover for Columbanus to go to a mere second monastic site. But this glosses over the personality of Columbanus himself. If he were just doing what everyone else did, he would have become a faceless entity to history rather than a singular individual. Columbanus, whatever may be said about him, was emphatically not just another young Irish monk.

Perhaps there was something special in Columbanus' nature that made him unwilling to be satisfied with his current level of accomplishment. His career was driven by a constant desire to do better, and more. He may have outgrown Sinell and Cleenish, or he may have wanted, as he would say years later in another context, "a more severer precept." He was a true wandering spirit, but not in an aimless fashion. Rather, he was constantly pressing on toward some higher mark. That pressing passion would take him not just from Cleenish but from every abode he established in Western Europe.

His first journey from the watery fastness of Cleenish was to the northeast and Belfast Lough where, only three or four years earlier, St. Comgall, another of Finnian of Clonard's pupils, had founded a new monastery called Bangor. Comgall had previously also established a monastery in Lough Erne, the mysterious *Insula Custodaria* of the sources, where he had developed a reputation for extreme ascetic demands. Comgall, a farmer turned monk, had first studied under St. Fintan of Cloneenagh, reputedly the most demanding of all Irish monastic taskmasters. Fintan was so severe with himself that he was said to eat only withered barley and drink water mixed with clay. While this might sound preposterously harsh to us, there are those even today who drink water mixed with bentonite clay as a method for removing toxins from the system. It could be that everything that sounds brutal to us was not always detrimental to the monks, many of whom lived to be quite elderly in an age before antibiotics and the assorted blessings of modern medicine.

Comgall apparently fully agreed with Fintan's emphasis on severity. The sources reveal that when he began his first monastic settlement at *Insula Custodaria*, no fewer than seven monks died from the extreme rigors he imposed there. Rumors even circulated that when Comgall died, years later in great agony, some whispered that the old abbot was simply getting a taste of what he had long inflicted on others. So it seems that Comgall left *Insula Custodaria* to try a fresh start at Bangor, one still rigorous but not so lethal. This appears to have happened in 558, perhaps a year or two before Columbanus showed up at Cleenish. Comgall's reputation for severity, lessened somewhat by the hard experience of tragedy but still formidable, might have been a drawing point for Columbanus and his restless quest for something better.

Whatever brought Columbanus to the new settlement at Bangor, it may be said fairly that he found a welcome home there. The monks traditionally offered hospitality to travelers, often washing the wayfarer's feet in imitation of Jesus' actions at the Last Supper. Their hospitality was no doubt even greater for one who was already a proven monk and professed a desire to join their monastic family.

The monastic family at Bangor was rapidly becoming a famous one. Situated on the south shore of Belfast Lough, the monastery was well placed to receive visitors. Monks and saints from all over Ireland came to Bangor regularly, and it was a prime departure point for visits to the continent, not just for monks but for merchants as well. Columbanus could not have known on that day in the early 560s when he arrived at Comgall's monastery that some day he too would make a journey to the continent. No, the young Columbanus must have believed he had found a permanent home—and for nearly thirty years it was so. The essence of Bangor, summed up a generation or two later in a document called *The Antiphonary of Bangor*, was simple, yet challenging: "Love Christ, hate wealth … piety toward the king of the sun and smoothness toward men."

We may assume that Columbanus was assigned an anamchara, or soul-friend while at Bangor. Comgall was a firm believer in the practice having said, upon the death of his own soul-friend that he felt "headless," because "a man without a soul-friend is a body without a head." Columbanus seems to have fit into this system early and well. We know little of the particulars of his long sojourn on the shores of Belfast Lough, but he was ordained a priest during that time—an uncommon accomplishment in the monasteries of that day—and seems to have risen to be Comgall's own choice to be the next abbot. He shone at Bangor. But a light hidden is not capable of radiance at all. Despite its location and roster of visitors, Bangor was not the place for Columbanus to brighten society. Radiance must glow in an outward direction, and the monastic world, such as that at Bangor, was designed to be inward-looking. The objective of monastic life was to withdraw from the world rather than engage in it. Later monasteries would actually build this point of view into their architecture. The cloisters, corridors walked by monks as they prayed, were constructed with no exterior windows, so that the monks would focus their attention inward on their own hearts and not on the lures of the outside world. It was a system built to avoid fame and influence, not to create it.

Even if Columbanus were to become the second abbot after Comgall's death, he still would have little chance of showing his abilities to the greater world. Comgall has come down to us only because he founded Bangor. We know relatively little about him other than his approximate life span (516–602), and that he was the son of a soldier who wanted the boy to follow in his military footsteps. The fame of Bangor produced Comgall's renown. But if Columbanus were to be his successor, would he not be famous as well? Anonymity seems to be the lot of those who succeed the famous. Most know, for example, that St. Peter was the first bishop of Rome, but fewer are aware that Linus was the second. Columbanus, no matter his talents, would likely be forgotten in the pageant of European history as the second abbot of Bangor—as was the actual man who ultimately did get the post in Columbanus' absence. This very absence is the defining event in Columbanus' life. It is what took him from the flourishing, yet parochial, milieu of Irish monasticism onto the world's stage as a major contributor to Western Civilization. It is to this absence that we must now turn.

White Martyrdom

As the year 590 approached, Columbanus was in his late forties and had been a monk for his entire adult life. He was the Abbot Comgall's favorite and he seemed destined to finish his life at Bangor. Late in the 580s, though, it seems that something began to stir in him. He began to think of the world outside, and gradually he became more and more impressed with the notion that he must leave Bangor and follow wherever his call might lead. In that era, when life expectancy was generally much shorter than today, a man of his age would be considered somewhat elderly. Did he become more aware of the inevitability of death and wish to "die" by leaving? Was it simply the continued manifestation of his wandering spirit? Several years and several countries away, he would preach a series of memorable sermons that likened human life to a roadway, and he would confess that he had been "always moving from the day of my birth." Even after nearly thirty years at Bangor, and, from all accounts, a happy and successful career there, Columbanus was drawn away. Multiple times in his letters to popes, bishops, and even his beloved companions, he referred to himself as a *perpetual pilgrim*. Therefore, the better question might not be "Why did he leave?" but "Why didn't he leave earlier?"

But what exactly was "leaving" for Columbanus? And did leaving have a special meaning for him quite apart from its meaning for the Christian world in general?

The Irish had been Christianized with remarkably little bloodshed. There were few, if any, hostile kings bent upon persecution such as the series of pagan reactions in Anglo-Saxon England after the death of the first English Christian king in 616. By Columbanus' day there was practically no violence between Christians and the remaining pagans. Therefore, the most exalted form of Christian witness for the age, the status of martyr, was largely unavailable to the Irish. While the word *martyr* itself originally meant "witness," the general public then, and still now, uses the term to describe one who has died for the faith. But it may be said that the Irish of Columbanus' day developed the term in a way more nearly true to its original meaning. If it really does mean "witness," then there must be other ways apart from physical death to become a martyr. By the sixth century there were three accepted versions of martyrdom open to would-be Irish saints. Columbanus experienced in turn two of the three.

The first, and the one that Columbanus missed, was the obvious one of death for the faith. Even though a Frankish king would later threaten him with this, Columbanus died of natural causes in his bed at the age of seventy-two. Owing to the shedding of blood involved in death for the faith, it became known as *red martyrdom*. But there could be other ways of dying for the faith by "dying" to the world. It was reckoned that a monk who left family and friends and voluntarily went into the wilderness as an anchorite, or even a member of a monastic community, was becoming a martyr as well. This ascetic lifestyle was called *glas*, variously translated as "green," "blue," or "pale" martyrdom. Why the ambiguity of terms? Colors are a notoriously subjective item; the word *glas* was much like that. In addition, it carried the meaning of "pale," which only further complicated the description of this type of martyrdom. Whatever its name, this was the call that Columbanus followed after leaving his distraught mother those many years ago in western Leinster.

But there was one more. Apparently beginning with St. Columba of Iona, the Irish embraced yet another, higher, form of sacrifice: white martyrdom. Columba, distraught at touching off a civil war in Ireland that took many lives, had accepted not just living the life of an exile in the wilderness, but leaving Ireland for good. This would be the ultimate "bloodless death," leaving home, kindred, and even your native land, never to return. It was, quite simply, abandoning everything a man loves for the sake of God. Recent studies have shown that this impulse had its origin in early Irish law. A severe punishment for a criminal was to be banished into the wilderness, somewhat like the green martyrdom of the monks, while the equivalent of capital punishment was to be banished from Ireland forever. In fact the same word was used interchangeably to describe a monk in voluntary exile and a criminal in a forced one: *peregrinus* in Latin, and *alither* in Irish. It may be that "outcast" most nearly captures the meaning of the terms. The three versions of martyrdom appear in the Cambrai Homily, written in Ireland in the late 600s and preserved on the continent from at least the 760s. The text explained that "this is white martyrdom to man, when he separates for the sake of God from everything he loves." Columbanus' white martyrdom was the severe and permanent renunciation of all that he knew and loved—even Bangor and his master, Comgall. This version of white martyrdom exerted a stronger and stronger appeal for Columbanus as his years at Bangor rolled by.

The Request

At some point prior to 590, Columbanus approached Comgall and asked permission to depart into this exiled martyrdom. Comgall rejected his request out of hand. It is easy to assume he did so because he feared losing his star monk and handpicked successor. This may have been so, but there was another factor as well. Comgall was wrestling with his own unfulfilled call. As he would later admit, he had felt the urge toward white martyrdom but had stifled it in favor of developing Bangor into one of the preeminent monasteries in Ireland. Therefore, he may have been predisposed to reject anyone else's proposal toward white martyrdom. It is said that even when St. Mochuda, also known as St. Carthach, came to him to ask his advice on white martyrdom, Comgall talked him out of it and sent him back home. If Comgall would do this to a monk from outside the Bangor community, he would surely never let Columbanus, an ordained priest and renowned scholar, sail away. Columbanus, despite his fiery disposition, was always obedient to his recognized superiors just as he expected full obedience from subordinates. But in Columbanus, persistence coexisted with obedience. We don't know how many times he requested permission to leave, but we do know that the old abbot did eventually relent. Columbanus would at last have his wish, to embark into the great unknown of white martyrdom.

But was it really unknown? The word used for his journey was *peregrinatio*, usually translated "pilgrimage." But this seems to miss the point, or at least mislead the reader. Maribel Dietz's study on religious travel in Late Antiquity notes that pilgrimage is generally taken to mean an organized trip to a definite place with a return expected. The peregrinus on a white martyrdom journey would neither know his end destination nor expect ever to return. So the peregrinus was, in effect, not only an outcast but a wanderer, banished from his homeland but with an itinerary and destination known only to God. In fact it might be said that the journey *was* the destination. A common theme in Columbanus' surviving sermons is that of life as a roadway. Columbanus didn't just see himself as "always moving from the day of (his) birth," but thought all people were like "travelers and pilgrims (*peregrini*) in the world." His biographer Jonas uses a biblical reference to make this point. Columbanus, he said, was following the same type of call given by God to Abraham in the Book of Genesis: "Leave your country, your people ... and go to the land I will show you." The Irish would call this type of pilgrimage *peregrinatio pro amore Christo*, or "pilgrimage for the love of Christ," and it would be a permanent state. Dee Dyas, author of a fascinating study on medieval pilgrimage, has explained that this white martyrdom was a type of life pilgrimage, not a discrete journey to a designated site with a return expected, but living one's life in exiled service to God.

One might wonder what exactly the purpose of this white martyrdom was. If it were merely wandering through this world, there was plenty of room for that in Ireland. If this martyrdom required leaving the homeland, why did Columbanus set his course for the continent and not the closer portions of the British Isles? Here Jonas, and many who deal with the issue today, read Columbanus' motives in light of his later career. Years later, after drawing many locals to his way of life and even spending several years trying to convert pagan tribesmen at the headwaters of the Rhine, Columbanus could fairly be called a missionary. But was that his intention when he set out from Bangor in 590? Jonas unabashedly portrays him in this light. Comgall was said to have relented and allowed him to go because of "the necessities of others" so that

Columbanus "might win glorious triumphs for the good of others." Yet even after years in exile Columbanus would only say, in what he thought was a farewell letter to his monks, that while he "loved the salvation of many," he loved it no more than "seclusion for myself," and that "these are longings in me rather than achievements."

If the journey was not a missionary enterprise from the outset, what was it? One line of explanation may be found in the organizing principle of Comgall's Bangor. Whenever one of the abbot's monks finished his clerical training, as did Columbanus himself, he was ordered to become *pater aliorum*, or "a father to others." Comgall appears to have trained his best and brightest monks specifically to lead ecclesiastical families. Comgall didn't just govern Bangor, he also had associated foundations at Colerain and at Tyree. These were led by a *praepositus*, or specially authorized "under-abbot." Whether Comgall wanted Columbanus to become one of these for yet another Irish branch monastery or whether he wanted him to be his actual successor, the point remains: He most definitely would not want Columbanus sailing off over the blue waves and into a white martyrdom. But perhaps Columbanus saw becoming a father to others as a natural part of this martyrdom. Taking companions with him to found a new monastic family on the continent seems to have been a more pressing motivation than converting pagans or even reviving religion among previously Christian peoples. If true, this would explain several mysterious twists and turns in Columbanus' continental journey.

Off to the Continent

Whatever the motive, we do know that Comgall allowed twelve companions from the monastery at Bangor to go with Columbanus as he launched from the shore of Belfast Lough. Posterity has recorded their names. Some will appear only on this trip, others will carry on Columbanus' work in such a glorious way as to attain lasting historical fame. The twelve, a thoroughly biblical number for disciples, were Attala, a younger monk also named Columbanus, Cummain, Domgal, Eogain, Eunan, Gall, Gurgano, Libran, Lua, Sigisbert, and Waldoleno. The presence of Germanic names such as the last two can be taken as proof that monks from the continent were already coming to Ireland to study even in the sixth century. Attala would succeed Columbanus as an abbot, and Gall would become a saint and the namesake founder of one of the most famous monasteries in European history.

This doughty band would likely have carried little with them since having minimal material goods was a way of life for them already. It is thought that they might have had skin bags for milk or water, hearth cakes, a concoction of hardened flour and water paste a bit like the hardtack of the American frontier, and, quite appropriately for the literate Irish monks, books of the Gospels, Psalms, and suitable hymns. Their vessel, most likely a curragh, was not much more than a wooden frame secured by iron nails, covered with ox-hides, and with the joints smeared with pitch and rosin to achieve watertightness. Flimsy as the vessel may seem, particularly when at the mercy of the tempestuous waters it would sail, the curragh was able to flex with the pounding of the waves and survive where other more rigid boats might not.

Jonas says little of their journey, noting that the trip was dangerous but that since "the spirit of the all-merciful judge was with them," they were able to sail "quickly with a smooth sea and favorable wind to the coast of Brittany." The ease of the journey has not been called into question—it is possible, though difficult, to catch an easy voyage south over the Irish Sea—but the fact that they went directly to Brittany has aroused skepticism. Most scholars believe the party stopped over in the southwestern peninsula of Britain at Cornwall before proceeding to Brittany. This itinerary again raises the question of motivation. If, as Jonas stresses, Columbanus' group was bound for missionary work, why not stay in Cornwall? And if they were only looking to found new monasteries with themselves as a nucleus, once again the question arises: Why not do that in Cornwall? If Cornwall were not sufficiently "heathen" to offer a mission field, it should be Christian enough to provide additional monks for a new foundation. Either way, it would seem a suitable destination.

The general take on this is that Cornwall was quite Christian, as was the adjacent land that would later be called Wales. So no missions were needed there. Since the British Church in these areas was notorious for a lack of missionary outreach to the growing Anglo-Saxon presence to their east, the situation offered little scope for missions to these pagan invaders. The land was also well populated with monasteries, making it a poor choice for that effort as well. This seems to make sense in that much of Irish monasticism itself had been heavily connected to the work of Welsh saints, and possibly directly inspired by them. Comgall's master, Finnian of Clonard, had formulated much of his monastic system while in Wales, and Columbanus himself referred to the Welsh saint Gildas as the source of much of his monastic structure. Cornwall and Wales to the north were at least as well stocked with saints and monasteries as Ireland itself and therefore not suitable for a white martyrdom consisting of monastic planting. So it was off to Brittany for the band of monastic brothers.

Landing on the Continent

Many think the ship put in near St. Malo on the Breton coast. A village called St. Colombe seems to mark the spot today. Jonas says they rested here for a while "to recover their strength." Apparently even a smooth voyage was a taxing one in the late sixth century. The men were said to have "discussed their plans anxiously." Indeed they well might have. Brittany was a tumultuous region in the post-Roman world. Originally a part of Gaul called Armorica, Brittany had been heavily populated by refugees from Britain following the Roman government's decision to no longer defend the isles after 410. So many Britons migrated there that the area was literally transformed into a lesser Britain, hence the name *Brittany*. But more than the name changed. The region would be a volatile and independent one for the entire period of the Early Middle Ages, following a different path than the rest of Gaul.

Even though Gregory of Tours reports that Brittany came under Frankish domination after the reign of Clovis (481–511), the record shows that the Bretons were violently independent in actual practice. Ruled by counts, from the old Roman military position of *comes*, the Bretons had a fractious form of government based on a bitter rivalry within the comital family. In the years before Columbanus arrived, one count, Chanao, killed three of his brothers and was actively hunting down the fourth, Macliaw, when he was finally dissuaded by means of a trick. Macliaw had himself buried alive with a small reed hole for breathing. When Chanao's assassins arrived, they were told Macliaw was dead and shown his grave as proof. After a celebratory drink on the grave, the assassins left, and Macliaw was dug up. His luck ran out later when another Breton chieftain that he had betrayed and driven from his lands came back to kill him. The murderously kaleidoscopic turn of Brittany's politics makes it a fascinating—and often baffling—subject for historians to this very day.

But one thing can be ascertained clearly: The Bretons exerted constant military pressure against the principal cities of the Atlantic Coast of Gaul. A typical scenario would have the Bretons invading eastward to take Rennes and south to seize Nantes, the former a key city astride trade routes, and the latter the port at the mouth of the Loire River that received most of the seaborne commerce from the British Isles. In this scenario, which occurred most recently in the very year that Columbanus arrived, the Franks would then launch a counterattack and punish the Bretons. The Bretons would promise to behave, the Franks would leave, and then the Bretons would forsake their promises starting the cycle again soon thereafter. In every way Brittany was indeed a separate world from the Frankish domains to the east. Jonas affirms this separation when he records that Columbanus and his men finally "decided to enter the land of Gaul" as they left. The wild frontier region of Brittany was no longer considered a part of the whole of old Gaul. But if not a part of Gaul, why not stay there? Once again scholars focus on the idea that Brittany had many monasteries and monks, so was no better a candidate for Columbanus' expedition than was Cornwall or Wales. Very near the group's landing spot was the headquarters of one of the more famous of sixth-century holy men, St. Samson of Dol. Behind this line of reasoning lies an important supposition about the group: that they were not missionaries or monastic entrepreneurs, but were simply looking for a "deserted place" to set up their own community worship. And even a deserted place would need the protecting hand of royal authority: a commodity lacking in the tumultuous Brittany. For this, they turned eastward into Gaul proper.

Leaving Brittany that same year of 590, the monastic troupe traveled almost due east some 300 miles to Rheims, one of the key cities in Frankish Gaul and the baptism site of Clovis, the first Frankish king to accept Christianity. The cathedral at Rheims would be the official coronation spot for French kings until the end of the monarchy in the nineteenth century. It was a long and arduous journey, perhaps a bit easier than a comparable one in Ireland due to the surviving remains

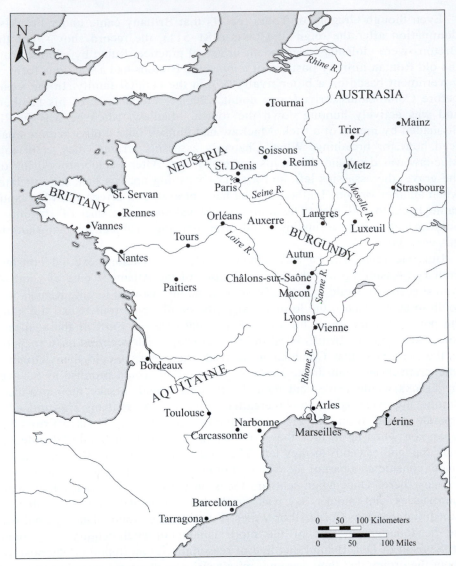

Map 5.1 Columbanus in Gaul 590–613 AD

of the Roman road system, but certainly equally as difficult. Whether or not the band of brothers had a particular destination in mind is not known. Jonas portrays them as preaching every step of the way and exhibiting "modesty and moderation, meekness and mildness." So winning a group might be thought to have simply stayed at any one of the many cities between Brittany and Rheims but they journeyed on. Did this itinerary offer no suitable deserted sites for their monastery? Or were they not as welcome to the local authorities as Jonas implies? Whatever compelled them, it took them deep into the heart of the land of the Merovingians.

6

Among the Merovingians

In many ways there could be no stranger land for these Irish monks to enter. If Brittany was not suitable to them, one wonders what made the Frankish ruled portions of Gaul better. Jonas, writing as usual with a specific agenda in mind, portrays this land as one where "the Christian faith had almost departed." For years scholars accepted this dire evaluation at face value. Only recently have studies shown it to be an overstatement. Gaul indeed had great ecclesiastical and political problems in this era, but so did the whole of Western Europe. The land would not be strange and forbidding to the white martyrs from Ireland because of the barbarous nature of local customs. The Irish themselves still participated in many of the more repulsive practices of that type of society. As already noted, an Irish king, contemporary with Columbanus and a professed Christian, still practiced the taking of the head of his slain enemies as trophies of war and it would be a century later before St. Adamnan would persuade the Irish church to forbid the slaughter of women in combat. Both Irish and Frankish cultures were heavily tinged with barbarism. It was not so much the culture as the chronic instability in the Gallic government and Church that made things dangerous for the *peregrini* from "the edge of the world." Gaul at this time was awash with swirling cultural change, royal feuds, and desperate power struggles as the blending of Roman and Germanic cultures took place.

The blending had begun in earnest in the early 400s, when a Germanic grouping of tribes collectively called the Franks had moved south from their settlements in modern-day Belgium into what would be northern and central France. They apparently were still divided into several subtribes—the Salian, Sicambrian, and Ripuarian Franks, among others—and were ruled by kings. An early one, Merovech, or *Meroveus* in Latin, was so significant that he gave his name to the Frankish line of kings that would rule until the mid-eighth century: the Merovingians.

We must not, however, think of these newcomers to Roman territory as unaware of Roman culture. The long generations of contact along the borders of the civilized Roman world had allowed for a great deal of cultural give and take. Many things we think of as purely German—sausage, for example—were introduced to the tribes by Roman merchants and soldiers. Even some Germanic names were mere combinations of Latin and German. The name *Kaufmann* is a union of the Latin *caupere*, meaning "to trade" and the German *mann*, or "one who does." By the late fourth century, so many barbarians had been hired into the regular Roman forces that the word *barbarus* became a synonym for *soldier*.

When the invasions began, the barbarians did not sweep over Roman Gaul with the intention of destroying all they encountered. Instead, it seems that they mostly wanted to become as the Romans. The familiarity with Roman culture produced by the years of interaction convinced the barbarians that Rome had much to offer. Recent studies in prosopography, or "collective biography," where a class of people rather than just an individual is studied to find common attributes, have shown that barbarians tried very hard to fit into the Roman social scheme, often intermarrying with key local families and even changing their names to Latin ones. Recent scholarship suggests that the issue of the barbarians supposedly taking one third of the land from the defeated Roman estate holders, which conjures up visions of the invaders violently dispossessing the helpless victims of conquest, now has been shown to be a taxation shift only. Rather than taking the land, the invaders appear simply to have taken the taxation allotment earmarked for defense—which the barbarians now provided. The upheaval of the barbarian invasions was indeed enormous and lasting, but apparently not as severe as previously thought.

This situation may explain the eventual melding of Roman and Frankish societies into something that would become French, but that blending was still in process by the time Columbanus arrived. It would be years later that Gaul would become known as *Francia*, or the land of the Franks, on its way to becoming "France." Complicating the matter further and adding to the uncertainty and danger was the presence of many other barbarian tribes in the land. The Franks may have become dominant by virtue of their aggressive military behavior, but they were by no means the only contributor to the blending of barbarian and Roman culture. There were pockets of Alans, a kindred people to the Persians settled in northern Gaul as defenders of Rome, as well as whole regions populated by other barbarian tribes: Suevi; Alamanni; and most notably in southeastern Gaul, the Burgundians. All this was superimposed on a Roman Gaul that, while mostly homogenous culturally, was already a mix of Celtic and aboriginal peoples. The unity of Roman government had, along with the enticing amenities of Roman culture such as public baths, roads, aqueducts and the like, held it all together. Now that was gone and in its place was a nearly constant struggle for control among any who could muster sufficient troops.

The Merovingian Rule

The royal Frankish house of the Merovingians moved to the fore in this confused scenario, but that too had its complicating factors. Many barbarian tribes, the Franks included, used a form of inheritance designed to give each son a full share of the patrimony. This type of inheritance, called partible inheritance, was sensible when dealing with flocks of sheep or herds of cattle. But as some of the barbarians left their pastoral lifestyles and became farmers, dividing up the estate was no longer an attractive option. After several generations an heir might expect to inherit a smaller and smaller parcel of land. It made sense to keep the estate intact and give it to only one heir. This was the general trend among the Franks. They seem to have been in the process of dropping partible inheritance in favor of primogeniture, or leaving the estate to the firstborn son.

Among the Merovingian royal house, however, partible inheritance still reigned. Generation after generation, any Merovingian king who could unify Gaul under his rule would then leave equal portions of the land to each surviving son. Therefore, the kingdom would break up only to reunite and break up again. The unpredictable trend was made even more dangerous by the natural rivalry between royal siblings that often took a most unnaturally lethal turn. Brother would often plot against brother, uncle against nephew, and even queens against queens.

Sometimes these plots could border on the ridiculous. One royal brother invited another over for a meal in order to kill him, only to have the plan fall apart when the assassins, hidden behind a curtain, were detected by their feet sticking out from under the drapery. The powerful Frankish king Clovis, the first to unify Gaul under Frankish rule and the first to be baptized a Christian, methodically accomplished the killing of all rival members of his kindred and then held a public meeting where he lamented the fact that he was now like an orphan without a family. It was thought that he did this supreme act of hypocrisy in order to find out if any other relatives remained so that he could dispatch them as well. As one scholar of the early twentieth century summed it up, "it was an age of grossness, cupidity, and violence" within the royal Merovingian family.

Out of this disunity Gaul eventually settled into three major Merovingian kingdoms: Austrasia, the northeastern lands along the Rhine; Neustria, the central portion; and Burgundy, the eastern and southeastern portion of Gaul that was once an independent kingdom but conquered by the Franks in 534. This apparent division was still complicated, however, by the tendency to class some key cities as separate from the main regions. While the old Roman cities were much shrunken, they still retained an aura of significance. These cities and their *territoria*, or surrounding countryside, could be held by the king of one Merovingian kingdom yet be located within another king's realm. At certain times, the city of Paris might be classified as a commonly held territory and thus off-limits to royal conquest. The end result of all this, especially when viewed from the perspective of Columbanus and his newly arrived band of peregrini, was that with almost every stretch of terrain they traversed, they would be moving from jurisdiction to jurisdiction.

Finding a Royal Patron

Even with the confusion and peril of crossing so many lines of governance, Columbanus and his companions apparently knew that the key to survival in this alien land was to seek out the reigning king and request approval for their monastic presence. But that was not as easy as it might seem. While each of the three major kingdoms had capitals, the Merovingian king, like so many others in the barbarian kingdoms that succeeded Rome, did not rule from a particular place. The seat of government, if it can be called such, was wherever the king was. As these early French kings loved to hunt in the expansive forests of Gaul, finding a Merovingian king and his court often came down to finding one of his favorite hunting lodges.

In this, Columbanus' group caught a bit of luck. It is apparent that Jonas knew little about this journey, as he describes Columbanus meeting with a king who had been dead for some fifteen years and in a kingdom he never ruled. Scholars solve this inaccuracy by deducing that Columbanus made his way to Rheims and found there King Guntram (d. 592), the last surviving son and heir of Chlotar I (r. 511–561). Chlotar had succeeded in imitating his famous father, Clovis, in unifying all Gaul. In fact, Chlotar has surpassed his father in that he controlled Burgundy, a feat Clovis never accomplished. By 590, three of Chlotar's four sons were dead, leaving Guntram as the elder Merovingian. But Guntram, who had inherited Burgundy, was childless. He was, however, big-hearted enough to want to protect the children of his dead brothers. In one dramatic moment, Guntram interrupted a solemn church ceremony to plead with the public assembled there to help him protect the lives of the young boys in his care. He knew that if the Frankish tendency to assassinate their kings were to continue unchecked, the entire royal line might die out, leaving the land in chaos. Even though one of the boys, Childebert II, was approaching twenty years of age and ruling Austrasia, Guntram still exercised great influence there.

Guntram was quite impressed with the Irish band, because of "the greatness of (their) learning." Columbanus, who had been seeking a deserted place to set up his monastic community, was given leave to choose a site in the Vosges Mountains of Burgundy. There he found a ruined fortification called *Anagrates*, now called Annegray. He and his men set about to convert the ruins into an Irish monastic settlement with Guntram's full blessing. This should not be surprising since the royal Merovingians were almost always locked in a struggle with the Christian bishops for control of the Church. The kings could exercise some influence over the selection of bishops, but once chosen, bishops exerted their own independent power. One forceful Merovingian king was so impressed, or should we say disturbed, by the growing power of the bishops that he repeatedly complained publicly, "There is no one with any power left except the bishops in their cities." A king like Guntram would likely see the benefit of authorizing a religious group such as Columbanus' that would be apart from the control of the bishops. This would be a constant theme in Columbanus' sojourn in Gaul: as long as the monarchy approved of him and his group as a counterweight to Episcopal power, he was safe. Whenever this approval was withdrawn, he was quite vulnerable.

But for the next few years, even after Guntram died in 592, Columbanus enjoyed a prosperous stay in Burgundy. His monastery grew as locals flocked to the charismatic presence that his piety and learning shed in that troubled land. He was forced to open an additional center, this time at another previously inhabited site called *Luxovium*, destroyed by Attila and the Huns in 451, and now known as Luxeuil, and later a third at *Fontanas*, modern Fontaines. All three were within only a few miles of one another and therefore Columbanus himself was capable of supervising them directly, using the same model that Comgall had used for the daughter monasteries of Bangor. The flourishing enterprise could not but threaten the local bishops who would see their hold over the populace diminishing as the popularity of these foreign newcomers grew. "People streamed in from all directions" to Columbanus' monasteries, as Jonas relates, including "children of the nobles."

Columbanus' cave retreat near Fontaines in the Vosge Mountains. The cleft in the rock in the background was inhabited by a bear when the saint arrived. Columbanus ordered the beast to leave, and he complied.

These productive days would ultimately be undone by the malevolent force of one of the longest-running and most vicious feuds in European history. Columbanus would be drawn into it against his will, but true to his personality, once so engaged he would not shrink from confrontation. The feud had been set in motion nearly a quarter century before Columbanus arrived in Gaul and would have nearly another quarter century to go before completing its blood-soaked course. It all began with a royal marriage.

The Feud

Back in 567, the sons of Chlotar, although nominally Christian, were bringing disrepute on their reigns by their loose marriage practices. The kings would have many wives and mistresses, often servant girls or any attractive and available women in the kingdom. In this unstable situation one of the brother kings, Sigebert of Austrasia, decided to break the pattern by marrying the daughter of Athanagild,

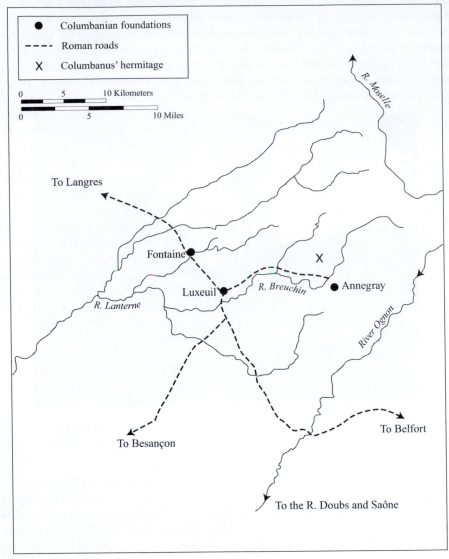

Map 6.1 The Vosges Monastic Foundations

king of Visigothic Spain. The bride's name was *Brunhilda*, and she was probably in her late teens, reputedly very beautiful, and a great means for cementing an alliance between the Frankish and Visigothic royal houses. The young queen was so popular in Gaul that Sigebert's brother, Chilperic, although already married and with a low-born mistress named *Fredegund*, who would become one of the most bloodthirsty characters in a most bloodthirsty age, determined to imitate his brother and marry his own Visigothic bride. Chilperic repudiated his mistress and brought Brunhilda's older sister Galswintha north to be his queen. But soon he returned to Fredegund and "someone" had Galswintha strangled. The furious Brunhilda blamed the mistress, Fredegund, and the feud was on. But rather than being merely a struggle between two women, this vendetta involved the kingdoms of Merovingian Gaul—and it endured generationally for nearly fifty years.

By the time Columbanus arrived in 590, Sigebert had been assassinated at the instigation of Fredegund in 575, and Chilperic himself had likewise been dispatched in 584. In both cases the assassins used a favorite Frankish weapon, the *scramasax*, a single-edged long knife often smeared with poison in the blade's groove. When each of the two kings was killed, the widow would flee for protection to the one dependable royal brother, Guntram, for refuge. As matters stood when Columbanus arrived at Rheims, Austrasia was ruled by Childebert II (570–595), the son of Sigebert and Brunhilda; Neustria by Chlotar II (584–629), the son of Chilperic and Fredegund; and King Guntram, now over sixty, ruled Burgundy and tried to mediate between the two warring factions.

As chaotically dangerous as this situation was, Columbanus seemed to fit right in—at first. All sides of the royal feud could see the benefit of befriending this holy man from Ireland, and it appears that for about twelve years all was well. Even the death of Guntram in 592, Childebert II in 595, and Fredegund herself, in 596 failed to upset the relationship between the Irish monk and the bloodthirsty royals. Brunhilda simply continued her dominance through her grandsons, Theudebert II in Austrasia, and Theuderic in Burgundy, while Chlotar II strengthened his rule in Austrasia. In a way, Columbanus' monasteries seemed "above the fray" of the incessant Merovingian wars. All that was to change, however, and with the same frightening swiftness that often marked the shifts in Merovingian politics.

Concubines, Not Queens

Brunhilda had been the power behind the throne for her two young grandsons, who were age ten and eight when their father died. But shortly after the year 600, when the eldest, Theudebert, was turning fifteen, there was an abrupt change of government in the northern kingdom of Austrasia. Fifteen was the traditional coming of age number for a Frankish monarch, and Theudebert, allied with key nobles, drove his grandmother out and took control of the kingdom. It was a situation that was all too familiar to the queen. Years earlier, when her own son was a minor and her husband dead by an assassin's hand, a coalition of nobles had thwarted her attempt to govern Austrasia. They had told her bluntly to stand aside because "you held regal power when your husband was alive. Now your son is on the throne, and his kingdom is under our control, not yours." The ongoing struggle of her life, as Brunhilda would see it, was one that involved her maintaining a hold on power by any means.

Fleeing Austrasia, Brunhilda went to her last base of support, that of her younger grandson, Theuderic of Burgundy. She was, however, determined not to make the same mistake twice. Nothing, or no one, was to take her power away in Burgundy. Knowing that Theuderic would soon become fifteen as well, she focused her attention on keeping the position of queen all to herself. Her older grandson had a queen and that made her an unnecessary ornament at court. If Brunhilda could keep her younger grandson from officially marrying, then she could wield power as the "queen mother." So, she actively encouraged the young man, barely a teenager, to keep concubines rather than take a legitimate wife. When nature took its course, and the concubines began to produce sons, Brunhilda wanted them recognized as heirs to the throne. She apparently felt confident that she could control her male descendants as long as they were not influenced by other women holding the royal status of queen. At this point Columbanus, a man so serious about sexual chastity and propriety that he had built his entire life's calling on it, could no longer remain neutral in Merovingian politics.

The ignition of this struggle began as young King Theuderic made a habit of visiting the Irish holy man for counsel. That by itself would pose enough of a threat to Brunhilda's influence to cause trouble, but the situation was even worse than that. It was not only that Theuderic was listening to Columbanus, but that Columbanus was giving him advice directly contrary to Brunhilda's plan. The Irish monk admonished the young king to quit his sexual laxity and marry a legitimate queen. As Jonas phrased it, Columbanus urged him to "satisfy himself with the comforts of a lawful wife, in order to beget royal children from an honored queen, and not bastards by his concubines." This characteristically blunt advice would infuriate Brunhilda. What was far worse for her, the impressionable Theuderic agreed.

There followed several years of tension among the Irish abbot, the young king, and the queen grandmother. Some scholars see Columbanus' growing conflicts with the Gallic bishops as indicative of the weakening protective relationship that the royals had long granted him. Brunhilda, for her part, apparently felt that Columbanus was too popular to confront directly. The issue drifted first one way, then another. At one point Brunhilda was forced to agree that Theuderic actually marry a Visigothic princess, a young girl named *Ermenberga*, and dismiss his concubines. Columbanus greeted this news with joy, but it was not to be. After the young princess came north to the Burgundian capital of Metz, she was put aside, deprived of the rich dowry she brought, and ultimately sent back to Spain with the marriage never consummated. Brunhilda and Theuderic had chosen the path of power and lust at the very moment of Columbanus' triumph.

We don't know if Columbanus asked for a meeting with Brunhilda to settle this issue or if she requested it. What we do know is that the Irishman went to see the queen grandmother at one of the forest estates in her royal domain, an old Roman villa near Autun called *Brocariaca*. It was here that the "cold war" between the two erupted into something much hotter. Conveniently, Theuderic was out hunting, as was the passion of Merovingian kings. So the confrontation would take place without the young king who so frequently wavered between his love of his grandmother and his deep respect for Columbanus. When Columbanus appeared in the royal residence hall, Brunhilda shepherded the four illegitimate children of Theuderic to the front and demanded the Irish saint bless them. The act was not without precedent. Brunhilda's other grandson, Theudebert of Austrasia, had been born of a concubine and duly baptized by a Frankish bishop. By asking the popular Irishman to bless the children, Brunhilda no doubt thought either she could disarm Columbanus by securing his blessing—after all, how could he continue to oppose Theuderic's lifestyle if he blessed the outcome of those very actions?—or, failing that, she could show him to be a harsh, old man who took out his spite on innocent children.

Jonas depicts Columbanus as gathering members of the Frankish nobility to his monasteries in great numbers. This would certainly seem to be borne out by the many brothers of Frankish descent who carried on his work after his death. But there is another verification of Columbanus' popularity with the Frankish public: Brunhilda's insistence that the Irish holy man bless her great grandsons as legitimate kings. Had Columbanus been a marginal, isolated figure with a limited scope of influence among the public, Brunhilda would scarcely have been interested in what the Irishman thought. After all, his very existence in Gaul was dependent on royal good pleasure. He should be clamoring to acclaim Brunhilda's great grandsons as future kings in order to maintain his protected position. But it was she who would do the asking. This strange man with his band of peregrini was apparently becoming a major force—all the more because he was not a player in the crass politics of the Merovingian Church. Columbanus could not be bought. His approval would not be a cynical ploy but a genuine one, and therefore would make genuine the boy-kings he blessed.

We don't know if Columbanus considered all of this as he spoke his reply. We do know from his letter to a church council that he was aware of his own tendency to speak rashly and later regret it. Perhaps his reply focused more on the one phrase in the queen's demand: "These are the king's sons." That made the issue a national, political one rather than a simple request to bless bright-faced toddlers. Whatever the thought process, or lack of one, Columbanus blurted out a devastating answer: "Know that these boys will never bear the royal scepter, for they were begotten in sin." The meeting broke up immediately. As the Irish abbot strode from the building, it was said a loud cracking noise was heard. It was a suitable metaphor for the break between the Merovingian queen and the Irish monk.

Once the protective royal hand was removed, events swirled quickly and dangerously. Brunhilda's initial ploy was to blockade Columbanus' three monasteries at Annegray, Luxeuil, and Fontaines. Her edict stipulated that the monks be confined to their monastic lands and that no one should have any contact with them whatsoever. This was intolerable to Columbanus, who still believed that Theuderic would listen to him even if Brunhilda opposed it. Breaking the royal blockade, Columbanus went to visit Theuderic at one of his hunting lodges. Arriving at sunset, he announced his presence to the king by sending word that he would not enter the royal lodge. The king would have to come to him. Theuderic sent a finely prepared meal to the famished saint, apparently hoping to open negotiations on a hospitable note. The crusty, old saint refused the meal with the cutting remark that it was not right that his mouth be defiled by food from one who "shuts out the servant of God…from the dwellings of others." Legend has it that the dishes and goblets shattered when Columbanus made his refusal. Whether they did so supernaturally or by the anger of Columbanus is not recorded. This seemed like a high offense to the Merovingian world, but was in fact an old Irish protest tactic called *troscud*. When wanting to make a point against an opponent, an Irish monk would often fast against the offender, even to the near approach of death. This hunger strike, or troscud, was designed to shame the other side into some kind of concession and lead eventually to a solution of the dispute.

This dramatic ploy seems to have worked. Theuderic and Brunhilda hurried out the next morning to promise a lifting of the blockade and that the king would once again attempt to amend his lascivious ways. Columbanus returned to Luxeuil in triumph, seemingly unaware that his Irish tactic had been matched by a time-honored Merovingian one: breaking promises.

The conflict soon resumed with renewed ferocity. Vitriolic letters were exchanged and extreme threats communicated. At length Theuderic appeared at Luxeuil and proclaimed that Columbanus was in violation of "the customs of the country" by not allowing all who were Christians into the interior of the monastery. This was certainly true, since Irish monasteries had a triple layer of access: the outer for anyone; the more interior for monks and Christians; and the innermost part, called *sanctissimus*, only for the monks. A king, even a holy one—which Theuderic most evidently was not—could not enter the holiest area. This was new to Gaul. Later in a writing defending such practices, Columbanus would show his knowledge of Church law by citing the Council of Constantinople (367) and its ruling that monks could observe their own native customs when in "pagan" lands. Of course, Gaul was not pagan—at least in theory. So the dispute was not to be resolved.

The standoff escalated in a torrent of angry words. Theuderic warned Columbanus that he would make things very difficult for him. Columbanus shot back that if that were so, then Theuderic, his kingdom, and all his line would be destroyed. Theuderic sputtered that Columbanus was begging for "the crown of martyrdom," and exclaimed that he was not "foolish enough to commit such a crime." With this, the king departed, leaving his agents to arrest Columbanus and take him as a prisoner to Besançon. Apparently the king and Brunhilda were unsure what to do next, for there was a delay of several days while Columbanus, although under loose guard, performed several miraculous liberations of prisoners in that Burgundian city. After awhile Columbanus, noticing the laxity of his guards, simply walked away from the city and made his way back to Luxeuil.

The royal tandem of Brunhilda and Theuderic must have known that this escape was possible, and may have even wanted it to happen to further prove the Irish monk to be a violator of royal law. Now, when hearing of the "escape," they sent fresh detachments to rearrest him. The first contingent could not find Columbanus, although it is claimed that he was hiding in plain sight in the church vestibule. A second party was more successful and took the saint into custody. They told Columbanus that he was being shipped back to Ireland, a bit of information that would completely nullify his white martyrdom. Accordingly, he vowed that he would not go. Finally the men charged with the task convinced him that they would be killed if they failed in their mission. Supposedly out of sympathy for them, Columbanus relented and was packed off toward Nantes on the Atlantic coast of Gaul. Those among his monastic brothers who were Irish were expelled along with him. But it was not to be.

The party of exiles progressed in stages from Burgundy into the Loire Valley in central Gaul. On the journey Columbanus penned an emotional letter to those he left behind, assuming as he did that he would never see his monastic brothers again. As they followed the river west, Columbanus insisted on stopping at Tours to pay his respects to the shrine of St. Martin. When his captors informed him that this was forbidden, it was said the boat inexplicably nosed into a berth at the city dock and refused to budge. So Columbanus visited the tomb of the preeminent saint of Christian Europe. When the bishop, Leoparius, who was the successor of the historian-bishop Gregory of Tours, hospitably treated the party to a banquet, another of those tense moments that Columbanus' sharp tongue produced occurred. Leoparius asked, in seeming innocence, why Columbanus was returning to Ireland. The reply was shocking: "That dog, Theuderic has driven me away from the brethren." The problem with this emotional, yet honest, retort was that one of Theuderic's *leudes*, or trusted nobles, was at the table and took offense. When he expressed his objections, Columbanus repeated his prophetic threat that "Theuderic...and his children will die within three years and his entire family will be exterminated." As if to drive the point home, Columbanus instructed the noble to be certain to take this information back to Theuderic himself. Strangely, since this episode occurred in 610, the death of Theuderic and his sons did indeed come to pass by the year 613; a historical fact that has puzzled scholars ever since.

Finally arriving at the mouth of the Loire and the port city of Nantes, the ship assigned to carry the exiles back to Ireland was hit by a rogue wave in the harbor and stuck fast aground. After three days, the captain gave up trying to refloat the vessel and put the would-be exiles ashore. As one might predict in this age of miraculous accounts, as soon as that was done, the tide floated the vessel free and it went on its way. The detachment sent to exile the group was suitably impressed and broke off their mission leaving Columbanus and his friends free to depart. But where would they go? If they went back to Burgundy and their monastic houses at Luxeuil, Annegray, and Fontaines, they would surely be arrested again. The changing nature of Theudebert, king of Austrasia and Brunhilda's other grandson, made that kingdom an uncertain destination.

Theudebert might just as easily hand Columbanus over to Brunhilda as welcome him. The best choice seemed to be Neustria and its king Chlotar II. As the son of Fredegund, Brunhilda's archrival, Chlotar was the sworn enemy of both Theuderic and Theudebert. Perhaps the weary band of Irishmen could find sanctuary there. The destination was agreed upon, and the fugitive group turned northeast. Upon their arrival, Chlotar who "had already heard how the man of God had been persecuted by Brunhilda and Theuderic … received Columbanus as a veritable gift from heaven."

7

Battling the Bishops

The attempted expulsion of Columbanus and his brothers by the ruling house of Burgundy raises fundamental questions about the Irishman's entire career on the continent. Why did his very existence there depend on the Merovingians? Why wasn't his natural ally and constant support the Gallic Church with its leadership, the bishops? As Columbanus and his band traveled through Gaul on their initial journey to meet old King Guntram, there was ample opportunity for the various bishops they encountered to embrace them and their mission. Why did that not happen? In over twenty years of ministry in Gaul why are there no collegial friendships to record?

Of the three bishops mentioned by name in Jonas' *Life of Columbanus*, one, Suffronius of Nantes, is openly hostile to the saint, while Leoparius of Tours offers him hospitality only after he did reverence at the tomb of St. Martin, thereby validating Leoparius' power as curator-bishop of this great pilgrimage site. The third, poor Desiderius of Vienne, who like Columbanus had run afoul of Brunhilda and Theuderic, appears in the narrative only to be murdered at the royal command. Oddly, Jonas makes no mention of Columbanus being summoned to the Council of Chalon-sur-Saône in 602 to answer for certain irregularities of practice. Of all the bishops the Irishman met and interacted with, there is scant hint of it in Jonas' record.

The standard answer found in studies on the matter echoes the available evidence left in Columbanus' letters and sermons. It seems the points of contention were several Church practices that differed from Ireland to Gaul. By far the most serious was the question of the proper date for keeping Easter. While we might find this somewhat negotiable today, in the sixth century the correct date for Easter was a huge issue and a type of litmus test as to what was, and was not, true religion. The calculating of the date was tied up in the earliest Christian desire to differentiate the new faith from Judaism. Therefore, despite the historical fact that Christ's resurrection occurred in connection with the Jewish Passover, different cycles of reckoning Easter emerged. One worked on a nineteen-year cycle, while another was based on an eighty-four-year rotation. By 457, the Church scholar Victorinus had suggested a compromise that, although later revised again, was accepted by most of the Christian world. The Irish, however, maintained an older computation, so that Columbanus' practice

59

could be seen to be out of step with catholic, meaning "universal," policy. The Council of Orleans, meeting in 541 and representing the bishops of Gaul, had agreed that the Roman Easter, and not the Irish one, was to be followed.

The intricate logic and obscure mathematical and theological arguments behind this whole issue are truly mind-numbing and tempt the modern reader to assume that the dispute was just a type of smoke screen designed to mask other, more serious disagreements. This is both true and false. It is false in that the Church of this period really did consider Easter computation to be of great importance. Our point of view should not prevent us from seeing this as the Church saw it. But there is truth to the assumption that other issues were at stake, lurking under the surface.

Another seemingly minor issue was that of the monastic tonsure, or haircut. The way a monk cut his hair signified much more than fashion. Rather, it symbolized his calling and the lifestyle he would lead. The continental fashion was to shave the head leaving a ring of hair around the crown, calling to mind the crown of thorns that Christ wore on the cross. The Irish custom, somewhat like the ancient Celtic warriors, was to shave the hair in front and let it grow long in back. Perhaps this signified that the monks were like warriors for God. Once again individual preference was seen as destructive of the universal unity that the Church must have. So the followers of Columbanus could be hectored about their peculiar tonsure and accused of divisive practices. Later in his life Columbanus would refer to himself as a *bald-pate*, but we don't know if he was referring to his shaved head or the loss of hair that often accompanies aging.

A far more serious matter, curiously not mentioned explicitly in the sources, was the question of monastic control. After all, monasteries typically grew to be quite large and prosperous. If the bishops could control the monastic settlements in their dioceses, they would greatly enhance their authority and wealth. This appears to be exactly the situation in the Gallic Church. Even though monasticism dated back to the fourth century in Gaul—St. Martin himself founded Marmoutier on the Loire River in the 370s—by the sixth century the Gallic bishops had gained control of the monastic holdings. In this, the bishops were simply conforming to the Council of Chalcedon (451) that had ruled that every monk must be subject to a bishop—but only of one city, not as a collective body. Consequently, the sources bristle with accounts of abbots who were governed by their local bishop. Gregory of Tours, while praising a sainted abbot named *Senoch* in the vicinity of his own see of Tours, related how he had to upbraid the abbot for his arrogance. Senoch meekly took the criticism, "purged himself entirely of vanity" and therefore earned a place of honor in Gregory's *Life of the Fathers*. Another holy abbot, Vulfoliac, now known in France as St. Walfroy, led an exemplary life and was largely responsible for converting the barbarians living around the city of Trier on the Moselle River. He did, however, have the audacity to build a pillar upon which he liked to sit and pray in imitation of the renowned St. Simeon the Stylite who had done likewise in Antioch a century earlier. The local bishops decided Vulfoliac was wrong to do this, lured him off his pillar under some pretext or another, and destroyed the column. When the abbot returned, he wept in anguish but refused to go against the bishops' rulings saying, "it is considered a sin not to obey bishops." Monasticism was present in Gaul but only in a form that was tightly controlled by the bishops.

In this setting Columbanus' monastic vision would be shockingly different. His was an Irish one, in which monasteries were not only independent of Episcopal control but often overshadowed it as well. The Gallic bishops would understandably look askance at a stranger implanting an unaccountable monastic system in their midst, particularly in light of successful recruitment and rapid growth that Columbanian monasteries enjoyed. For every tract of land Columbanus reclaimed, for every monastic enrollee he counted, the Gallic bishops could see their share of authority in Gaul shrinking.

But it was not just the growing numbers of would-be monks that seemed threatening to the established Church. Gallic bishops did much more than pray and celebrate mass for their parishioners; they were in effect a sixth-century welfare system. The bishop was required to keep a household that was to be always open to the needy. This was regularly called the *domus ecclesiae*, or "church household," and it existed to serve the needs of the faithful. Church councils even forbade bishops from keeping dogs as pets in the belief that these four-legged friends might be tempted to bite the poor as they came for help. The bishop kept a table that was available to feed any who were hungry as long as they registered with him. These were called *matricularii*, "the registered ones," a term still used for college students who register at an institution of higher learning. The bishop was not just a religious leader but a patron for everyone in the diocese. It's no wonder that when a popular sixth-century bishop was threatened with removal from his Episcopal territory, or see, the people lined the road and chanted *Cur nos deseris, bone pater*? ("Why do you leave us, good father?"). The bishop was the father of cleric and layman alike. He was the dispenser of wealth and sustenance. Anything that seemed to encroach on this would be seen as a threat by the Church establishment.

While Columbanus' monasteries may seem to be for monks only, and thus no threat to the bishops, certain practices brought from Ireland caused immediate problems. In Ireland the monastery was the safest sanctuary for wealth. The monastic *termon*, or boundary, marked the site as a sacred sanctuary. So the lay people of the surrounding territory would place their valuables in the trustworthy hands of the monks for safekeeping. This "monastic bank" was not always inviolate, but was the best option for those trying to protect their portable wealth. We have proof that Columbanus brought this custom to the continent in the writings of Paul the Deacon, whose *History of the Lombards* was written in the eighth century. He described Columbanus' founding of Bobbio, his last great monastery, in Lombardy, and noted that "in this place also many possessions were bestowed by particular princes and Lombards." Since Columbanus' monasteries held the treasures of the laity, they also held their allegiance. Therefore, the question of monastic independence was much more than just a matter of governance over some isolated souls living by themselves *in desertis*, but a dangerous competing source of power. But this issue of monastic control was not immediately apparent when Columbanus first trekked from Brittany toward Rheims. There was something else at work against Columbanus from the very moment he began to move through Gaul.

Wanderers and False Prophets

Throughout the decade before he arrived, the land had been plagued by the appearance of numerous false prophets who typically would show up in a given town, impress the people with their apparent religious sanctity, oppose the established power of the bishop, and eventually be shown to be frauds. Gregory of Tours chronicled two of these outrageous episodes, in his city alone, one from 580, and the other in 587, a scant three years before Columbanus passed through Gaul.

In the first instance the imposter barged into Gregory's private quarters and berated the bishop for not reverencing properly his false relics. Later he went to Paris with "a mob of ruffians and peasant women" and disrupted a holy procession there. After cursing the Parisian bishop, he was locked up and eventually found to be a runaway slave. In the 587 event a false prophet named *Desiderius* claimed that messengers regularly carried news to him from the Apostles Peter and Paul. Desiderius ate scant food and wore a simple tunic with a goat's hair hood. This was calculated to give him an air of ascetic holiness, and the public embraced him enthusiastically, even though he ate lavishly in private. Finally, his falsity was discovered, and he was expelled never to be heard from again.

Gregory thought these false prophets to be a sure sign of the end times, and it is noteworthy that such characters tended to appear in conjunction with outbreaks of the plague. Fear can make a society desperate for the kind of answers a charlatan can claim to provide. As Gregory summed it up: "Quite a number of men now came forward in various parts of Gaul and … in their frenzy put it about that they were saints." The very year Columbanus landed, one of these deluded fellows even went so far as to claim to be the second coming of Christ, leading to his execution by Bishop Aurelius of Le Puy.

The situation was made more critical by the lack of a standard mechanism for determining who was a saint. In that era public opinion made saints. Further, a saint need not be dead to be acclaimed as such. While this informal system worked well for those, such as St. Martin, who were truly holy, there was always the danger that a false prophet might entice the people with "miracles" and be acknowledged as a saint before a correct appraisal of his saintliness could be established. In that nightmare scenario, one might have the creation of an "anti-saint," an instrument of evil rather than good. Understandably the bishops of Gaul were leery of any strange newcomers who appeared in their midst, failed to acknowledge their jurisdiction, worked signs and wonders, and drew large numbers of the public to themselves. In this light Columbanus and his group might appear to be just another false prophet with his henchmen in tow. To be sure this was only a first impression but, as the old cliché asserts, "You never get a second chance to make a first impression." It may be fair to say that Columbanus' initial impression on the Gallic bishops was never really replaced by a more favorable one.

Some Points of Agreement

In spite of the seemingly unrelieved conflicting points of view in this struggle, there were Columbanian practices that the bishops seemed to have accepted. The most famous is his advocacy of a novel approach to penance which would do so much to influence Western Church practices. Penance, the doing of a physical act of punishment to complete the forgiveness of sins, had a relatively recent emergence in Christian practice. It received a major boost, somewhat inadvertently, at the hands of St. Jerome (347–419). As Jerome translated the Bible into readable Latin in the early 400s, a work that became famous as the Vulgate Bible, he wrestled with choosing the proper Latin word for *sin*. He apparently rejected *crimen*, or "crime," as being too legalistic and settled on the word *peccatum* as a less judicial term. Peccatum, from which we get our modern words such as *impeccable* ("without fault") and *peccadilloes* ("minor faults"), still retained a certain legal connotation as well. If one committed a peccatum, one was held to have incurred both guilt (*culpa*) and punishment (*poena*). In a court of law this made perfect sense. If the accused confessed and showed remorse for his or her deed, he or she would be addressing his or her guilt—but would still have to do a prescribed punishment. It was, and is, certainly not enough to say one is sorry in a court of law. The penalty might be mitigated somewhat, but must be paid all the same.

Was "sin" like this? Did asking forgiveness take care of all that was required, or did a forgiven sinner also still have to do some sort of punishment, or penance? The Church eventually decided that a forgiven sinner must indeed do penance, and it became customary to do that publicly and only once. Consequently, the faithful put off this embarrassing and final penance until the last possible moment in life. However, one cannot know when the last possible moment actually might be. The end result of all this was that many people never did penance, and some enthusiastically sinned throughout life, believing that they would take care of everything in some later, final burst of penance. Bishops had very little control over the behavior of their flock under this kind of system.

So when Columbanus came to Gaul with an Irish model of penance, perhaps begun in his home monastery of Bangor, the Gallic bishops saw great merit in it. Why was this so? The Irish penance is sometimes called *tariffed penance* because it prescribed precise penitential measures equal to the exact sin in question. It was much like a price scale, or tariff. While this is certainly true, there was much more to the system's appeal than that. Irish penance as practiced by Columbanus was literally a daily endeavor. The Irish abbot believed that the faithful—not just the monks in his care, but the laity too— should examine themselves daily and see if there was any sin that needed forgiveness, and, of course, penance. There was to be no waiting until one final reckoning. The reckoning was to be a quotidian, or daily, thing.

Why would the bishops, already highly suspicious of this foreigner and threatened by his monastic structure, accept this? A look at the old, public penance and its requirements will make the choice for private "tariffed" penance obvious. In the old system, the penitent would confess to his bishop in private, but after that everything else was calculated to bring attention, if not outright ridicule on the one undergoing penance. The penitent's hair was cropped short; he was required to dress in somber garb, often a goat's hair shirt for maximum discomfort, abstain from wine and meat (anyone refusing these foodstuffs at table was routinely asked if they were a monk, cleric, or a penitent), and be cut off from fellowship with other Christians. During the prescribed penance he could attend church but could not receive the Eucharist, had to leave with the catechumens (those not yet baptized), had to sit in the rear of the church, and while everyone else stood during the service, he must kneel. All these requirements marked the penitent in his every action and acted as a constant reminder of his fallen status. Further, the negativism did not stop when the required penance was completed. The penitent was considered "reconciled," but still was not allowed to resume relations with his spouse, was forbidden ever to be a cleric, could never serve in the army nor resume government service if a ruler and the facts of his penance were to be noted on his tombstone.

Why would anyone undergo this roster of stigmas? According to the Church teaching of the era, if one failed to do the required penance for lesser sins, the so-called *peccata minuta*, he would suffer in *ignis purgatorius*, "the fire of purgatory." This would not be forever as its duration was limited according to the accumulated sins of the forgiven sinner, but would be very intense, as anyone who has ever experienced even one second in a flame can attest. Should one not do the required penance for deadly sins, called *peccata captitalia*, "capital sins," he would be damned forever. By the sixth century, peccata minuta could be satisfied by good deeds apart from official, public penance, but peccata capitalia required the full treatment. So strenuous and off-putting was this structure that the faithful understandably waited as late in life as possible to fulfill this obligation. The fact that it could be done only once, therefore making a relapse into sin a final, irreconcilable event, made it even more essential that it be postponed until the very end.

In contrast, the Irish system, while harsh in its punishments, was private and therefore not so permanently damaging to reputation and livelihood. It was geared to the addressing of daily sins, and thus was repeatable. Since it was daily and universal, it also had the benefit of leaving the penitent free to resume his normal life, marriage, government, military service, and the like, providing the penitent avoided further sin. The clergy would not only hear the confession but prescribe the penance themselves. So it was that the bishops appreciated this daily control over the laity that the Irish system offered, while the laity themselves appreciated the reasonableness of the scheme. It's no wonder that this new process caught on and became the basis for Church practice in the Christian world of the Middle Ages and beyond.

Columbanus also brought a different monastic rule to Gaul. But apart from quibbles about hairstyle and sharp disagreement about the correct date for Easter, the bishops seemed unconcerned with the regulations imposed on these Irish-style monks. There are at least two reasons for this. First, there were many different monastic "rules" ongoing in Gaul at that time. The famous Rule of St. Benedict, which would one day become the standard for Western monasticism, was only one of several in use during Columbanus' day. A standard interpretation of the issue of Celtic versus Benedictine monastic rules is to show them in desperate competition, as was the case in England nearly half a century after Columbanus' death. That may be true for the situation in Britain leading up to the Synod of Whitby (664), but was not the case in Gaul in the sixth century. In fact Columbanus' monasteries often seem to have used a "mixed rule" that was a combination of his work and Benedict's. So congenial were the two to each other that Columbanus' many monastic foundations are often credited with actually spreading the popularity of Benedict's rule rather than opposing it.

An Appeal to the Pope

Despite the points of agreement, such as on matters of penance and their indifference to specific monastic rules, the bishops still had plenty of reasons to attack once the restraining hand of royal protection was removed. They held all the real power but were seemingly unaware of Columbanus' willingness to risk everything to defend his position. After a decade in Gaul, in 600, the bishops demanded he conform to established Gallic practice. Columbanus not only refused, but responded to their pressure by going over their heads to one of the towering figures of Church history, Pope Gregory I "the Great" (r. 590–604). We have Columbanus' letter to the pontiff, but neither the charges that prompted it, nor the pope's reply. Some scholars believe the Gallic Church felt itself outside the pope's control and they see Columbanus' bringing him into the controversy as a turning point in reuniting Gaul with the rest of Christendom. The case for a "national" church feeling independent and outside papal control can be made for other barbarian kingdoms such as Visigothic Spain. However, Columbanus' elaborate praise of the pope, and his pledge that Ireland had always followed the papal lead, does not necessarily encourage one to believe that reintegrating Gaul into the mainstream was his intention. He always saw his monasteries and his own presence in Gaul as a type of extraterritoriality, a little bit of Ireland transplanted into a strange land. What he appeared to want from Pope Gregory was an agreement on the dispute so he could demonstrate the Gallic bishops to be "outside" the orthodox fold and not him.

But Columbanus did not simply react to the bishops' charges on Easter and proper tonsure. He went, as was his personality, on the offensive by asking the pope what he thought of "those bishops ... who ordain uncanonically, that is for hire." Pointing out that "many ... are known to be such in this province," he passed on the Irish opinion that these men were *simoniacs* (or buyers and sellers of Church offices—a practice named after Simon Magus who tried to buy the Holy Spirit in the Book of Acts) and *pestes*, "plagues." Columbanus was not simply leveling baseless charges. The very year he arrived in Gaul, back in 590, a Syrian merchant named *Eusebius*, a layman, had bribed his way into the Bishopric of Paris and promptly filled all the clerical offices with his family and loyal friends. Rather than submit to the bishops' pressure, Columbanus fought back furiously. As we don't know Gregory's reply, we can only guess at whether the pope agreed with the Irishman's accusations. It apparently took the bishops nearly two years to bring formal charges against Columbanus, since the next confrontation occurred in 602, when he was ordered to appear at the Council of Chalon-sur-Saône. The site of this council was in Burgundy, and Burgundy was the home base of Brunhilda and Theuderic.

Columbanus simply refused to appear. Was he convinced that, as an Irish abbot ruling Irish-style monasteries in a foreign land, he was not under the jurisdiction of these Gallic bishops? That certainly would be consistent with his general position. But he did do the bishops the courtesy of sending them a lengthy letter in which he was at once conciliatory and confrontational. Starting with sarcasm, he observed that it was a marvelous thing that so many bishops should meet just about him and his practices. He then chided them that they ought to have regular councils, as good church procedure required, but they did not. Then he turned conciliatory, asking "Let Gaul, I pray, contain us side by side." This may not be the simple plea for coexistence that it appears, but a restatement of his view that he should be allowed to be as Irish as he pleased in his own monasteries whether they were in another land or not. As a parting shot, he wondered if "those who often look at women and who more often quarrel and grow angry over the riches of the world" could be effective Christians at all, much less worthy bishops. In closing, he could not resist one more jab at the general moral weakness of his opponents. The war was definitely under way.

Seven years later, as Brunhilda, Theuderic, and their new allies the bishops turned up the pressure, Columbanus wrote to the pope again. Only this time he didn't know the pope's name. All he knew was that Gregory had died and someone had ascended to the chair of St. Peter. One can feel the desperation in Columbanus' letter as he made an appeal to what amounted to an "unknown" pope. Following Gregory's death in March 604, the papacy had been held in turn by Sabinianus from 604 through 606, and Boniface III in the year 607. We cannot know which of these men was pope when the letter was written because we are not certain of the exact date of its writing. But Columbanus begged whoever was pope to intervene, asking once again that he be allowed to maintain his Irish customs in Gaul even though bluntly admitted, "we accept no rules of your Frankish friends." His monks would "dwell in seclusion, harming no one," an apparent offer to limit or cease his outreach to Frankish nobles and the local laity in general. But Columbanus must have known that he could no more stop his charismatic outreach among the masses, impressed by one so sincere and bold, than he could cease being himself.

All this was, of course, in vain as the wheels of discord moved relentlessly toward his expulsion from Gaul. By this time, Brunhilda and Theuderic had withdrawn their protective hands. Columbanus soon found himself voyaging down the Loire, bound for Nantes and passage back to Ireland. What prevented this expulsion, the "refusal" of the ship to budge from port, was seen as divine intervention. While the antagonistic bishop of Nantes, Suffronius, is not mentioned by name in the aftermath of this miracle, "all aided the man of God with gifts and food." A miracle may have saved him for the moment, but the bishops and their royal patrons could certainly be counted on to try again. That's why he made his way to a friendlier court, that of Chlotar II at Soissons. Perhaps here he could find the peace he needed to continue creating the monastic bits of Ireland that he longed to implant.

The Miraculous Missionary

When Columbanus fled to Soissons, he was received, so says Jonas, as "a veritable gift from heaven" by Chlotar II. Once again this is a testimony to the growing popularity of the Irish saint. Now Chlotar could say that he, and not his royal rivals, Theudebert and Theuderic, was favored by Columbanus' presence. But this "gift from heaven" was still the same sharp-tongued *scottius iracundus* as always. It was not long before Columbanus began to point out the sins of the king and his court and despite Jonas' glossing over the dispute as "such as could hardly fail to exist at a king's court," the tension began to mount. While there, Columbanus did cheer Chlotar with his often-repeated prophecy of doom for Theuderic and his house. At length, when the royal brothers Theuderic and Theudebert went to war, both asked Chlotar for an alliance. Columbanus persuaded the Neustrian king to stay out of the fracas since "within three years he would receive both kingdoms." Despite this favorable prediction, the king and the abbot apparently wore on each other. So it was with mixed feelings that Chlotar learned that Columbanus wanted to leave Neustria and journey eastward to Theudebert's kingdom of Austrasia. The Irishman wanted to skirt Burgundy to the north and cross the Alps to enter Italy. Since Theudebert had just made war on Theuderic and Brunhilda, Columbanus felt secure in going to Austrasia. Chlotar provided an escort of troops to safeguard the trip.

Theudebert, seeing a benefit in having the enemy of his brother and grandmother in court, also received the Irish contingent "joyfully." There had been a steady stream of Columbanian refugees coming to his court from Luxeuil, Fontaines, and Annegray, so Theudebert's kingdom was a type of haven for the fugitive saint. At ease in the capital city of Metz, Theudebert suggested that Columbanus' party "preach to the neighboring peoples." Perhaps he would rather Columbanus preach to pagans than to loose-living royals such as himself. The Austrasian kings had for generations experienced a love-hate relationship with the peoples beyond the Rhine, sometimes using them as effective allies in Merovingian wars and at other times fearing their ability to destroy the kingdom itself. If these people could be converted to Christianity, perhaps they might be more dependable and safer allies.

There was a precedent for this point of view. When Clovis was baptized as the first Christian king of the Franks in 495, Bishop Avitus of Vienne had written him, suggesting that he carry his new faith beyond the Rhine. Back in Ireland,

St. Columba of Iona had been commissioned to preach to the wild Picts of modern-day Scotland by the King of DalRiata, modern Argyll, to convert them and keep them from threatening his borders. Of course, it seems to have escaped these kings' notice that putatively Christian monarchs, such as themselves, still invaded and conquered other territories and kingdoms. But it was thought that should the barbarians become Christian, as coreligionists they might be easier to handle. Missionaries seemed to have real political and military value in these uncertain times. No doubt with a good deal of spirited negotiation, Columbanus and Theudebert agreed upon a target area for the enterprise.

Up the Rhine to the Pagans

So the hardy band of monks accepted the offer and left Metz, sailing downriver on the Moselle until it joined the Rhine at Koblenz. Then they began the arduous journey of more than 300 miles, rowing upstream against the current, all the way to Lake Constance (The Bodensee) at the headwaters of that mighty river. At that point they traversed the entire breadth of this beautiful freshwater lake all the way to the eastern end and a ruined, abandoned settlement called *Brigantia*, today known as Bregenz. Now Columbanus seemed an avowed missionary to those living beyond the Christian world. Had he not always been that?

Certainly Jonas portrays him as a true missionary. The saint is said to have gone to Gaul to "sow the seeds of salvation," and wherever he and his band "remained for a time in a house, all hearts were resolved to practice the faith more strictly." When Columbanus founded Luxeuil, Jonas tells us that "people streamed in from all directions in order to consecrate themselves to the practice of religion." He drew more than the common folk in this way. Jonas reported "the children of the nobles … strove to come thither." Columbanus' life is intertwined with many Frankish converts, a development that would ensure his legacy there even as it encroached on Episcopal control. The powerful Frankish Duke Waldelenus was so impressed with the holy power of the Irish saint that he dedicated his firstborn son to Columbanus' work and his second son, although also later a Duke, founded a monastery on the Columbanian model. Some of Columbanus' most faithful attendants and companions in Gaul were recent Frankish monastic recruits. Frankish names, such as *Theudegisel, Chagnoald*, and *Chamnoald*, are described as attendants and disciples. Frankish matrons, such as Theudemanda, opened their larders to him in recognition of his holy power.

This constant impact on any and all who seem to have come into contact with Columbanus has usually been portrayed by scholars as missionary activity. Yet the Irishman may not have had missions work as his principal motivation. Perhaps it was a different interpretation of "missions" that he had in mind.

We must not forget that what Columbanus brought to Gaul was a bit of Ireland, and in Ireland monastic communities were not strictly missionary enterprises. It is true that Irish monasteries were generally sited in spots that were accessible to the potential monks who would come. But there was also an element of isolation from the world that was often in evidence. The frequent resort to island monastic sites testifies to this approach, as does the habit of walling off the settlements with an earthen *vallum*. It seems a rare mix of accessibility for the new members, yet inaccessibility for the masses as a whole. Would-be monks, who wanted to withdraw from worldly things, were welcomed, but the settlements were not designed to convert the general populace.

That Columbanus viewed his calling in Gaul in this way is clear from his letters and even from the words of Jonas himself. Unlike St. Patrick, who had a recurring dream in which he saw the people of Ireland standing in a great wood imploring him to come and share his faith, Columbanus came to Gaul to seek monastic solitude. All his foundations, beginning with Annegray, were notable for their "entire loneliness." When the public flocked to this strange holy man and his disciples seeking healing, it was only after "he was unable to rid himself of their importunities" that he prayed for their needs. Even then he seems to have expected them to go back to their regular lives. Writing to the bishops at Châlon in 602, he begged them to allow him to "enjoy the silence of their woods and to live by the bones" of his departed brethren. Although he may have been merely downplaying his influence on the populace in order to quiet the bishops' worries about his encroachment on their power, other statements lead one to believe he really didn't seek mass conversion of the public. He repeatedly refers to his communities as places of seclusion, "which I have sought from overseas for the sake of my Lord." In his letter to the unknown pope he characterized his career as "dwelling in seclusion, harming no one." Later, writing from a broken heart at being expelled from Gaul, he confessed to his monastic brothers, "You know I love the salvation of many and seclusion for myself … but these are longings in me rather than achievements."

On the surface the throngs that were magnetically attracted to this novel man and his novel approach to religion look like the fruit of purposeful mission work. But as the great scholar of Merovingian Gaul, Pierre Riché has noted, this was an unexpected by-product of his actual intention to found monasteries. He was, in effect, an accidental missionary. His real intent, as it was back home in Ireland, was to create and offer special places where Christians might follow, in his words, "some still severer precept of the evangelical religion and apostolical tradition." Columbanus was a revivalist, seeking to call believers to a deeper faith, and not a missionary introducing heathens to a new belief system. All that was to change once he left Theudebert's court and rowed with his companions up the Rhine. Now he was intentionally setting out to share his faith with the barbarians in this remote region on the edge of Austrasia. And in so doing, something that had marked his entire career in Gaul, now more than twenty years in duration, would come into play in a critical fashion: miracles.

The Question of Miracles

The prevalence of miracles in the sources of Columbanus' day poses a real problem for our modern world. We are so attuned and accustomed to knowing the natural cause of unusual phenomena that we dismiss readily as mere superstition any and all mention of miracles in these early sources. Even those among us who might grant the possible existence of the miraculous are put off by the sheer volume of miraculous occurrences listed there. Miracles are by definition rare; the seldom intervention of the divine into the normal workings of the world. Thus, the overwhelming volume of the miraculous in writings of this period produces an equal reaction of skepticism. But this perspective, that miracles are the occasional supernatural intervention into the natural order, is the product of the later Middle Ages, some 600 years after Columbanus' day. In his time there was a completely different viewpoint on the miraculous. It had received its best expression in the writings of St. Augustine, which we know Columbanus had read.

Augustine did not see the miraculous as the "occasional," but as the normal. To him, all life was suffused with miracle and we only occasionally become aware of it. This occasional awareness would explain the rarity of miracles but, conversely, if miracles were truly all around, they should be seen, or realized, on a fairly frequent and numerous basis. The holier a person was, the more the surrounding miraculous world would be made perceivable. This corresponded well with the view of the age that there was no real separation between the natural and the supernatural. It was all one. This explains, as previously noted, why a Merovingian king could leave a letter on a dead saint's tomb and confidently expect a written answer. If there was this easy interchange between the natural and the supernatural, then miracles were merely confirmations of holiness. In writings about holy people, such as Columbanus, one might expect to see a profuse miraculous presence. That's also why the sources of this era rarely use the word *miracula* for the miraculous, preferring instead to use the word *signum*, or "sign." What we consider miracles, or the suspension of the rules of nature, were to them divine signals indicating to the spiritually perceptive the "true" condition of things. So when we read of a saint in the sixth and seventh centuries, we must be prepared to work through a full catalog of miraculous occurrences. It was certainly so with Columbanus.

Within the less than one thousand words of Jonas' *Life of Columbanus* that cover the period from the saint's arrival in Gaul to his landing at Bregenz, there are at least thirty-five miracles recorded. Many of them betray the stock descriptions of hagiography, often paralleling miracles from the New Testament as a way of connecting the saint to Jesus' life. Therefore, Columbanus is depicted as restoring sight to a blind man at Orléans by touching the man's eyes, casting out a demon from a Parisian by grasping his ear and striking his tongue, and healing "the wound with his saliva" when an axe head flew off and split open the forehead of a parish priest. Columbanus is also shown to imitate Jesus when he fed sixty hungry monks at Fontaines with "two loaves and a little beer," with twice as much left over as they had originally. But imitation was never self-glorification. Columbanus always prayed to God for the miracle and was quick to ascribe it to divine power rather than his own. When feeding those monks, he prayed "Christ Jesus ... do thou, who from five loaves satisfied five thousand men in the wilderness, multiply these loaves and this drink." The common error when dealing with the miraculous is to credit power to the agent rather than to the originating source. Columbanus was careful to give that credit to God. His admirers, as was so often the case with many saint cults of the age, were not nearly as careful, choosing instead to credit him.

The many miracles connected to Columbanus' career fall into readily identifiable categories. There were provision miracles, involving food or water appearing for his men, often including the generosity of neighboring believers who were divinely prompted to bring the supplies without knowing why. There were also healing miracles, involving sickness or injury, such as the grisly account of a monk with the good Frankish name *Theudegisel* who cut his finger with a sickle while harvesting. So severe was the wound that only a small strip of skin attached the dangling finger to the hand. Once again, Columbanus used his saliva to restore the finger to "its former health." Another, prevalent type of healing miracle, in this age that believed so staunchly in the interplay of nature and the supernatural, was the curing of the demon possessed. On his would-be exile journey, Columbanus healed "twelve demoniacs" at the aptly named village of Cure, yet another sufferer at Auxerre, an entire "band of mad men" at Orléans, a possessed woman at Nantes, as well as the previously mentioned demon-possessed man in Paris. The early church office of the exorcist was alive and well at the hands of this Irish saint.

There were also protection miracles such as the occasion when Columbanus was beset by barbarian bandits while meditating in the deep woods. Deciding that it would be better to be attacked by wild beasts which were innocent in their violence, than by such sinful men, Columbanus' fervent prayers were answered and a pack of wolves, rather than the barbarian raiders, approached but did not harm him. He was also protected against the "royal" type of wolves when Brunhilda sent men to arrest him at Luxeuil. The soldiers were unable to see the saint, although he sat calmly in plain sight in the church's vestibule reading a book. When he was at length arrested, one of the military escort sent to apprehend him tried to kill him with a lance only to have his arm paralyzed. When the man begged forgiveness, Columbanus "sent him home healed." But protection was not just for Columbanus himself. Boarding a boat at Nevers, a surly guard struck one of the saint's companions. Columbanus predicted the man would pay for the unprovoked attack with his life at that exact spot on the return journey. And so he did.

But one category of miracles stands out from the rest and reveals Columbanus to be what he always was: a son of Ireland. The Irish had long been noted for their love of nature and their conversion to Christianity did nothing to diminish that. It is a typically Irish custom to portray their saints as having a special relationship with the created world. This is in stark contrast to much of the continental literature that viewed the world as "the devil's playground" and nature in general as something to be rejected. The Irish appear to have enjoyed both the beauty and the usefulness of flora and fauna. Irish saints' lives teem with stories of holy men, women, and beasts working together as a type of return to how the world once was. St. Ciaran of Clonmacnoise frequently was visited by a stag that would lie in front of him so that he could use its horns as a reading stand, while a flock of wild ducks reportedly attended

St. Colman wherever he went. In fact this may be part of the creative tension found in Irish monasticism; the monks appreciated the very world they were denying themselves. Columbanus was certainly no exception. In a passage where Jonas portrays him as enjoying the squirrels that frolicked about his shoulders as he fasted and prayed in the wilderness, the biographer instructs the reader to "not wonder that the beasts and birds thus obeyed the command of the man of God." Animals "came immediately at his command and he stroked them with his hand." Columbanus, like so many other Irish saints, was well connected to the natural world.

Yet there was one creature that seemed to encounter Columbanus so frequently as to become almost a symbol of his career: the bear. When looking for a quiet spot to pray some seven miles away from his growing monastery at Annegray, Columbanus found a discrete little cave. Once inside he was shocked to find a bear had made its den there. Columbanus "ordered the beast to depart" and, miraculously, it did. This cave den became the saint's favorite retreat. At Luxeuil some time later, Columbanus discovered a bear preparing to devour a freshly killed stag. Apparently emboldened by his earlier victory over the other bear, Columbanus "ordered it not to injure the hide which was needed for shoes." The bear meekly complied, and "drooping its head, left the body without a murmur." The monks sent to strip the deerskin noticed that no birds or other wild beasts had dared to approach the stag's body. Later, far away at Bregenz, Columbanus had yet a third encounter with a "fierce" bear. The beast was raiding the monks' apple supply so Columbanus directed his assistant to divide the cache, one portion for the bear and a larger portion for the monks. His command over the bear was such that the beast left the restricted apples untouched. For some reason, Columbanus seemed to have a special affinity for bear control. When Columbanus is depicted in art, he is often shown as dominant over a gentled bear. The ability to relate to, and command, the birds of the air and the beasts of the wild, even the most ferocious, was a Celtic attribute that Columbanus participated in to the fullest.

There were, of necessity in a catalog of wonders this large, some miracles difficult to categorize, yet impressive all the same. Columbanus interceded for a barren couple; obtained freedom for condemned prisoners at Besançon by his prayers; and prevented one of his young monks, an Irishman also named *Columbanus*, from dying by virtue of his intercessory prayers. Columbanus also seemed to have miraculous power over boats. Perhaps this is merely a corollary of his white martyrdom where the boat was to take him wherever God wished. The circumstances of his abortive exile from Gaul necessitated that he travel extensively by boat down the Loire and out into the Bay of Biscay. His prayers forced the riverboat to dock at Tours against the commands of his guards, and the ship designated to send him back to Ireland miraculously refused to float off a sandbar. Events associated with his voyages were also the subject of miracles. When his companions were robbed of their meager possessions while at Tours, Columbanus, the living saint, prayed to St. Martin, the dead saint and protector of the city of Tours, that he give justice to his men. Naturally, the culprits were stricken with great torments and quickly returned the stolen goods, begging for pardon as they did. It seemed that Columbanus moved in a world of the miraculous wherever he went. How many were added in by Jonas to certify his subject as a saint, one can only speculate.

At Bregenz

But when the holy man and his party got to Bregenz the miracles seem to have taken a different direction. While there are still the standard wonders, the purpose of the miracles seems to shift from confirmation to evangelism. This, indeed, is at the heart of the scholarly debate about medieval miracles that continues today: Were they meant to confirm the sanctity of the saint and his followers, or were they meant to impress unbelievers into belief? The interchangeable use of the word *signum*, or "sign," with the word *miracula*, offers little help in making a determination. In Columbanus' case the issue is clouded further. Many of his miracles prior to his overt missionary efforts at Bregenz were ones that persuaded believers to consecrate themselves to monastic life. This was certainly a type of conversion, if conversion is meant to signify a change in life direction. This was, of course, somewhat different from that of a pagan rejecting his old beliefs in favor of Christianity. The "evangelism" miracles prior to Bregenz were calls to Christians to seek a deeper commitment, while those at Bregenz were directed to nonbelievers.

The most famous, and colorful, of these episodes occurred early on in the sojourn at Bregenz. Even though Columbanus had agreed, sight unseen, with Theudebert that Bregenz would be a good place to settle, the actual spot "did not wholly please" the irascible Irish saint. But, as Jonas tells us, "he decided to remain in order to spread the faith among the people." In this irritable state of mind he ventured out among the pagans to win them over. Passing through the forests, he stumbled upon a religious ceremony that involved a huge cask of beer. Rather than preach to them, or even join the revelers in a drink—since Columbanus' men were not unacquainted with beer—he decided to wreck their ceremony. Discovering that the beer was a drink offering to Wodan, the chief Germanic God, he reportedly "breathed on the cask" smashing it to pieces. Jonas explains this bizarre event by saying that the cask exploded because Columbanus had expelled the Devil from it. He then records the Germans' laconic reaction: "The heathens … said Columbanus had a strong breath." Despite their few words, "many were converted" in the aftermath of this powerful demonstration.

Apparently the missionary enterprise went well during the approximately eighteen months Columbanus was at Bregenz. His close companion, Gall, was gifted with language abilities and aided him greatly in reaching the natives in their own tongue. So enthusiastic did the once reluctant Columbanus become that he even entertained thoughts of moving on into Slavic territories farther east. It seems that the Irish wanderer could not stay put even when crowned with success. Only a divinely inspired dream featuring "an angel of the Lord" persuaded him to remain.

Leaving Bregenz

Dreams or no, the kaleidoscopic turning of Merovingian politics finally forced Columbanus to leave Bregenz. Brunhilda and Theuderic were once again on the prowl and by 612, felt themselves strong enough to attack Theudebert in Austrasia. Hearing of the impending war, Columbanus visited his royal patron, Theudebert, and offered him what must have seemed irrational advice. The saint counseled this Merovingian monarch to step down from his throne before the war would begin and enter a monastery. It looks as though Columbanus was trying to save Theudebert from the defeat and death that he had foreseen. But to the king's ears, it must have sounded absurd. Despite the advice from so friendly a saint, Theudebert took his army into the field against his brother and grandmother at Tolbiac, modern-day Zulpich. This city had played a major role in Merovingian history before. It was here that Clovis defeated the Alamanni only after calling on the Christian God for help. That victory led directly to the Frank king's baptism. But on this day in 612, Theudebert was defeated and the arch-enemies of Columbanus, Brunhilda and Theuderic, took control of Austrasia, including the budding missionary outpost of Bregenz.

Here Jonas records a peculiar example of Columbanus' miraculous powers. At the precise hour of the struggle, the saint was sitting on the trunk of a felled oak in the forest reading a book. Falling asleep he dreamed of the exact outcome of the battle. When he awoke he told his companion what he had seen in the dream. Urged by the monk to pray for the friendly Theudebert to win, he refused, saying "the Just Judge has already determined what He wills concerning them." Apparently Columbanus was reluctant to pray for God's intervention on his own behalf in the matter of Merovingian politics.

In this Columbanus represents a bit of a departure from typical Late Antique thinking. It's just one of the many ways Columbanus stands as a transitional figure between the ancient and medieval world. The accepted view on war was one that believed God would intervene on the battlefield in favor of the just side. References to this intervention as *velox ultio Dei*, or "the swift judgment of God," dot the literature. God was not seen as some distant judge, tabulating offenses for an eventual Day of Reckoning, but was thought to be capable of striking down transgressors immediately whether they committed some heinous crime such as homicide or a lesser one such as breaking the prohibition against Sabbath labor. Therefore, He could be appealed to via fervent prayer from righteous lips and persuaded to grant victory to the correct side. Once again the prevalent view on the joining of nature and the supernatural made this seem a sensible course of action. As early as 394, in the hotly contested Roman civil war between the Christian emperor Theodosius and his pagan opponent, Eugenius, the emperor had prayed all night on a bluff overlooking the battlefield at Frigidus and his desperate, losing army. When the emperor concluded his prayer with the shout, "Where now is the god of Theodosius?" a sudden, howling wind materialized and disorganized the opposing forces so much that the Christian side won. A half century later, Bishop Germanus of Auxerre, visiting Britain, prayed so effectively while witnessing a clash between the Britons and the Anglo-Saxons that the miraculous battlefield verdict was forever called "The Alleluia Victory."

But Columbanus did not merely choose to leave unused a standard means for obtaining military victory. He refused to pray not because he believed Theudebert to be unjust, even though that king had rejected his advice to abdicate his throne. Theuderic and Brunhilda were unjust, as Columbanus knew all too well from personal experience, so Theudebert would look quite good in comparison. The real reason he refused to pray for Theudebert's victory may be that he was taking a different perspective on war. This point of view was similar to the Old Testament position exemplified by Joshua just before the Battle of Jericho. Upon meeting an angel of the Lord, who carried an unsheathed sword, Joshua asked him if he were on the Israelites' side. The angel answered that it was more important for the Israelites to be on God's side than for God to be on theirs. By saying that "the Just Judge" had already determined the outcome, Columbanus might have been acknowledging that military victory, like the rain, falls on the just and unjust alike. Winners in battle may or may not be righteous, a point of view that would take many centuries to mature, but one day carry the field.

In the aftermath of the battle, Theudebert was captured, sent to a monastery just as Columbanus had advised, and then soon executed. But Columbanus was becoming wise to the ways of Merovingian politics at this point, and he knew it was time to leave what was now certain to become hostile territory. He had originally entertained notions of going to Rome even before he became sidetracked to mission work with the Germans. Now seemed like a wise time to make good on that desire.

But as Columbanus left, one of the most painful confrontations of his life occurred. His beloved companion, Gall, so successful in his work with the Germans, professed sickness and asked to remain at Bregenz. Columbanus never let sickness stand in the way of work or travel. At one point he had commanded his monks, so weak they could barely stand, to rise from their sick beds to work the fields. Of course, they were healed as soon as they obeyed. Gall, no matter how beloved, would not be an exception. Columbanus ordered him to travel and when he refused, the saint cursed him with the judgment that he not celebrate mass as long as Columbanus was alive. So Gall remained behind in this chastened state to continue his work, apparently unmolested by Brunhilda and Theuderic, leaving a great monastic foundation that bears his name: St. Gallen.

Even as Columbanus left Bregenz for Rome, he received an amazing offer from the Lombards, the Germanic conquerors of northern Italy. They wanted him to settle there. The official word came from their king, Agilulf, but the whole enterprise was the work of one of the most fascinating women in European history, Queen Theudelinda. So it was to Lombardy, which was, after all, on the way to Rome, that Columbanus and his band now turned.

Landing in Lombardy

As Columbanus traveled south through the Alpine passes, he could not have known that he was embarking on the final journey of his storied career. If, as he often said in his sermons, life was a highway, then these were to be the final miles of the trip. That year of 612, he was approaching seventy yet still so full of vitality that he could work with the hardiest of his companions. It took hardiness beyond that of a typical seventy-year-old just to make the trip, considering it involved an ascent through the mountains of more than 7,000 feet. But as he and his men descended to what was rapidly being called the Plain of Lombardy after its recent conquerors, Columbanus was once again entering an alien world. The Merovingians had been treacherous, but they had been Catholic. The Lombards would be of uncertain religion, yet steadfastly friendly to the vagabond Irishman and his monastic brothers.

The Lombards were originally called the Winnili until, as legend says, they were renamed by the god Wotan who, remarking in surprise at the sudden increase in their army's size, asked "Who are these Langobards (or "long-beards")?" Some scholars suggest that their name may just as well have come from a long pole weapon they used, but it seems true that the Lombards apparently favored shaving their heads in back and letting the hair of the crown and front of the head grow long on either side. Then the hair was parted in the middle, giving it the appearance of a beard. In the legend, the Lombard women had pulled their hair down over their cheeks in order to impersonate the men and give the army the appearance of greater numbers. Whatever the true origin of the Lombard name, and there are several contenders, they became one of the numerous Germanic tribes who dismembered the Western Roman Empire. In fact the Lombards were the last major tribe to invade, crossing the Alps in the spring of 568, and occupying northern Italy thereafter.

But the Lombards were different in several respects from many of the other Germanic tribes of the invasion period. First of all, they were a composite tribe. In some ways all Germanic tribes were larger, merged versions of smaller subtribes, but the Lombards were truly a mixed people. This grew out of their habit of incorporating defeated enemies into their population, even going to the extent of freeing captured slaves to become tribal members. The greatest Lombard historian, a mid-eighth century writer known as Paul the Deacon, notes that this policy was used to "increase the number of their warriors," but it shows a remarkable flexibility and openness not seen elsewhere.

This was not, however, as gentle a process as it might seem. One of the most bloodcurdling stories of barbarian Europe comes from this very time and practice. Alboin, the robust, blond Lombard king who led his people into Italy, had earlier gone to war with another Germanic tribe called the Gepids. After a fierce battle, Alboin succeeded in defeating and killing the Gepid king Cunimund. The victorious Lombard took the dead king's daughter, Rosamund, as his bride as well as the head of Cunimund as a war trophy. In spite of this, the Gepid survivors were incorporated into the Lombard host. Later having made a drinking cup of Cunimund's head, Alboin had the preposterous bad taste to offer it to Rosamund in order to drink a toast. Needless to say she was deeply offended at the thought of a celebratory drink from her father's skull and set about to plot, successfully as it turned out, Alboin's eventual assassination. Gruesome as all this is, it does illustrate that the Lombards picked up members of other tribes as they conquered their way into Italy, much like a snowball grows in size as it rolls downhill. The end result of this is that it is quite difficult to speak of the Lombards as if they were a homogeneous people.

Consequently, a second difference between the Lombards and other Germanic tribes comes into play. Historians usually class the Lombards with the Visigoths, Ostrogoths, Burgundians, and Vandals as barbarian tribes who were Arian Christians. The Arian heresy, named after the dissident Greek theologian Arius (d. 336), believed that Christ was created by God the Father. This appealed to barbarians who recognized that "the Son" should logically come after "the Father," but caused theological concern to those who felt that a created Christ could not be fully God. Throughout the fourth century, certain Roman emperors would officially accept Arianism, only to have their successors, depending on their doctrinal whims, condemn it once again. Arian missionaries, the most famous being Ulfilas (311–383), preached this belief to the Visigoths, a leading Germanic tribe. Ulfilas was half-Goth and half-Greek and had studied religion in the empire at a time when Arianism was considered orthodox. He possessed undeniable linguistic skills, becoming the first to translate portions of the Bible into Gothic, using purple-stained parchment inscribed with silver ink. He therefore was the creator of the first written version of a Germanic language. Ulfilas and his unknown associates were wildly successful in converting the Visigoths to Arianism. By some undocumented religious process, this particular version of heretical Christianity made its way into several other barbarian tribes as well during the next few generations. Meanwhile the fading Roman Empire had finally concluded that Arianism was indeed incorrect doctrine, and by 381, had conclusively declared it to be a heresy. That decision did not carry beyond the limits of the empire, however, and Arianism continued to percolate through the barbarian world.

So when the invasions actually came to pass, the invading Arian tribesmen were separated from their new subject peoples not only by culture but by religion as well. It is, however, inaccurate to consider the Lombards to be as Arian as their Gothic or Vandal contemporaries. The very fact of their mixed composition assured that many Lombards were in practice quite pagan, and a few were Catholic Christians. As a result one does not find the level of religious persecution in Lombardy as is found in Vandal North Africa or Visigothic Spain. Their heterogeneous composition made them by necessity, if not thoroughly tolerant, at least more open to persuasion.

Added to this was the Lombard tendency to abandon a central kingship and fragment into multiple governments under war leaders, or dukes. Many barbarian tribes broke their kingdoms into smaller pieces, the Franks being an excellent example of this practice, but those fragmentations were done as a function of inheritance within a chosen royal family. The Lombard model was not to fragment kingship among heirs but to reject the notion of kingship altogether and break the kingdom into as many as thirty-six separate political entities. As long as a powerful or charismatic king ruled, the nation was one. But whenever an uninspiring leader or a disputed succession arose, the possibility of shattering the nation was real. The rules of politics, as well as religion and culture itself, would be quite different in Lombardy for Columbanus and his companions.

But one similarity between the Lombards and other Germanic tribes was present to work in Columbanus' favor: the peace-weaving bride. It was common practice for the kings of one nation to marry a royal bride from another tribe as a way of cementing alliances and avoiding war. That's the origin of the kenning, or symbolic descriptive term, *peace-weaver* for these women—their marriage would literally weave peace between two potentially hostile peoples. In the Germanic cultures Columbanus encountered, this practice had existed for generations. Childeric (r. 458–465), the father of the Frankish king Clovis, had married a Thuringian princess, and Clovis himself married the Burgundian royal, Clotilde. Closer to Columbanus' day, both Chilperic and Sigebert had wedded Visigothic royal brides, although the former's murder of his new wife set in motion the feud between Brunhilda, the surviving Visigothic spouse, and Chilperic's descendants. The peace that was woven could, as with any fragile fabric, be torn apart by violence.

Generally, however, such unions were successful in their objective. Often the marriage was between royals of differing religions, with the result that the wife would conform to the beliefs of her new country. So Clotilde, an Arian, had no trouble becoming a Catholic as soon as her husband Clovis was converted from his paganism by Bishop Remigius of Rheims. But sometimes the wife would exert strong influence on her regal husband to change the tribe's religious affiliation. This was a tricky undertaking since the Germanic people tended to view their king as a mediator with their gods. The people believed that if the king changed the religion of his kingdom, dire calamity might befall. It was all part of the old practice called *blot*, common in the pagan tribal societies of northern Europe, that made the king the intermediary between the people and their gods. Therefore, the king could be replaced much more easily than the religion of the tribe. No matter what personal alteration of conviction a Germanic king might experience, he would often be very reluctant to go public with it out of fear of being deposed. Thus it was that Clovis, who normally feared nothing, was said to experience real trepidation before announcing his decision to be baptized a

Christian. And this blot practice kept the Burgundian king Gundobad from announcing his willingness to renounce his Arianism and become Catholic when otherwise convinced by Bishop Avitus of Vienne.

The Power of a Queen

Yet it did happen that foreign queens persuaded their husbands to change religious course. Clovis' great-granddaughter, Adalberg, was married to the Anglo-Saxon king of Kent, Aethelbehrt, and successfully convinced him to become Christian, thereby making his capital of Canterbury the seat of English Christianity to this very day. Clotilde herself had played a major role in persuading Clovis to drop his paganism in favor of the new Christian faith. This was the model that the queen of the Lombards aspired to in 612, when she instigated an invitation to Columbanus to come south and reside in her kingdom.

This remarkable lady was Theudelinda, a teenage Bavarian princess when she was married to the Lombard King Authari as yet another peace-weaving bride, sometime just before 590, the year Columbanus arrived in Gaul. The details of her courtship and marriage are elaborated by layers of romantic legend. Authari went disguised as a mere envoy to evaluate the prospective bride, and boldly made advances to her even though she thought him only an attendant rather than her fiancé-king. Offering her a cup of wine in hospitality, he stroked her face and then took her hand and ran it across his own profile. The blushing princess reasoned that only a king would have the nerve to be so forward to one already promised. He finally revealed his true identity after an act of egotistical bravado, driving an ax amazingly deep into a tree and crowing "Authari is wont to strike such a blow as this!" The young queen was to have less than two years to be this tempestuous and overbearing king's consort before an assassination made her a widow. But for some reason, perhaps because she was a woman of impressive charisma, or that she was seen as useful to certain factions at the Lombard court, or both, Theudelinda exercised immense power in Lombardy apparently from the moment she arrived.

The Lombard kings, like other Germanic royals, had no one capital but spent quite a bit of time in *Ticinum*, modern-day Pavia, on the Ticino River about five miles from that river's confluence with the mighty Po. This city was apparently much more defensible than Milan, some fifteen miles to the north. The Lombard treasury was at Pavia, but Milan was not to be ignored. Milan, old Roman *Mediolanum*, had been a key city in Roman history, even serving as the western capital after 286. It was here that the Emperor Constantine was crowned and issued his famous edict granting toleration to Christianity in February 313. It was the home of St. Ambrose (340–397), the mentor of St. Augustine, corrector of the Emperor Theodosius, and arguably the founder of the idea of saint cults by his moving of the burial sites of the martyrs Gervasius and Protasius to a place of honor under the high altar of his cathedral in 386. A city of this heritage drew the Lombard court like a magnet, and Theudelinda understood that paying homage to Milan would make her popular among the Roman subjects of the

Lombards. To that end she endowed richly a church at *Modicia*, modern Monza, just northeast of the outskirts of Milan. She may have been a foreign-born peace-weaver, but this teenage queen knew well how to obtain and use power.

When her husband Authari was poisoned on September 5, 590, the young queen might have expected to be shipped back to Bavaria and oblivion while the Lombards wrangled over whether or not to even have a replacement king. After all, Authari had reigned for less than seven years and had taken the throne after a decade of rule by multiple dukes. But, shockingly, neither Theudelinda's ouster nor the Lombard political fragmentation took place. One of the most amazing events in Germanic history happened instead. Theudelinda, this newcomer, outsider, and Catholic, was not only allowed to remain as queen— "because Queen Theudelinda pleased the Langobards greatly" as the chronicle tersely states—but she was asked to pick out her new king from among the leading men of the tribe. She chose Agilulf, Duke of Turin and an avowed Arian, to be her husband and monarch. Perhaps Agilulf was the leader of the faction that had toppled Authari, or perhaps he was just the strongest and most aggressive of the various Lombard dukes. Because of Theudelinda's choice, he became the first Lombard king to wear The Iron Crown, said to include a nail from the True Cross brought back from the Holy Land three centuries earlier by St. Helena, the Christian emperor Constantine's mother. He would rule wisely and with great strength. But rarely has a queen consort exercised so much control over the actual ruler. It would soon become clear that she exercised that power mightily on behalf of Catholicism and against Arianism. This campaign of hers would culminate more than twenty years later with the invitation to Columbanus to settle near Pavia.

Prior to Columbanus' coming, Theudelinda had corresponded repeatedly with Pope Gregory the Great, receiving handwritten copies of the pope's writings as a token of their friendship. Gregory considered Theudelinda "undoubtedly devoted to the faith of Christ and conspicuous in good works," and was overjoyed when she brokered a much-needed peace treaty between the city of Rome and the Lombards. Besides founding churches, she also persuaded Agilulf to restore all the property of the Catholics that had been confiscated by his predecessors. Finally, in late 602, the Queen gave birth to a son, the heir to the throne, Adaloald (who would reign under her influence for more than a decade after Agilulf's eventual death).

Barbarian kings were noted for polygamy, or sometimes "serial monogamy," as they married and discarded wives for convenience or political gain. But the queen who could provide a male heir, and thus ensure the *stirps regia*, or "royal stock," would be honored and kept. Theudelinda already had huge influence, now with the birth of Adaloald that influence would only grow. So, just as Clotilde had done with the Frankish king Clovis more than a century earlier, Theudelinda demanded that the baby be baptized as a Catholic rather than an Arian. It is a measure of her power that this was done at Easter in 603. Other barbarian queens had failed to persuade their husbands to allow baptism for their infant sons. Some scholars have concluded that this meant the Lombards had rejected Arianism. But given the uncertain nature of Lombard royal succession, there was no guarantee that Adaloald would ever reign. Allowing the apparent heir to the throne to be baptized as a Catholic Christian was a significant step, even if subsequent events proved the Lombards not yet ready to leave their Arian faith. When Columbanus was invited to Lombardy, the process of a Catholic victory over the Arian factions seemed well under way. All that was needed was a learned Irishman with demonstrated drawing power among the laity and nobility to inspire the king and his court to make the final move.

A Royal Patroness

So, Columbanus found a willing and powerful patroness when he went to the old Imperial city of Milan. Rather than a vindictive and murderous queen such as Brunhilda, Columbanus enjoyed a steadfast supporter in the person of Theudelinda. He immediately set to work preaching and writing against Arianism, an undertaking that would have cost him his life or at least sent him into exile under an Arian monarch who was not already considering a religious switch. It was therefore no surprise when, shortly after his arrival at court, Agilulf offered him the option of picking any place in Lombardy to establish a new monastery. A court functionary with a Roman name, *Jocundus*, suggested a ruined church dedicated to St. Peter in the Apennine Mountains. Columbanus always seemed to prefer to renovate ruined sites, from Annegray to Bregenz. This site, nestled by the hills near the River Trebbia, also suited his nostalgic tendency to mimic his homeland back in the Blackstairs Mountains of Leinster. It has also been suggested that this site, with a ruined church dedicated to the Prince of the Apostles rather than an old fort such as the one at Annegray, was symbolic to Columbanus. Much of his work on the Continent had been, in his view, the restoring of a ruined church by preaching a return to serious religion, a "still severer precept" as he phrased it. The rebuilding of the old church of St. Peter would be a microcosm of his efforts to rebuild the deteriorating Church of St. Peter in Christendom as a whole. His new monastic site, extending to a perimeter of about four miles, would be one more island of purity and light in a darkling religious landscape. The place was called *Bobium*, and Columbanus' monastery there would memorialize it as Bobbio.

Settling in, the monks were said to be supernaturally aided in felling and fashioning great log beams for the roof of the church. In a burst of hagiographic hyperbole, Jonas states that the elderly Columbanus lifted timbers that "thirty or forty men could scarcely carry." The establishment of Bobbio, as with Annegray, Luxeuil, and Fontaines, seemed to be blessed by divine assistance. All seemed well in this newly found haven, a feeling that was only reinforced by the arrival of a delegation from Chlotar, the king of Nuestria. The news was quite welcome to Columbanus although with a certain bloodcurdling sound to our ears. Theuderic had died, probably of dysentery, earlier in 613, not long after he and Brunhilda had disposed of Theudebert. Brunhilda had then done as she always did, simply taking the next generation of children to use as "king" in the now unified Austrasia and Burgundy. But this time significant numbers of the nobility were not supportive and failed to back the new boy-king Sigebert. Chlotar received word of the weakness and, recalling Columbanus' prophecy that he would one day rule over all of Gaul, launched a ferocious attack. The battle was decisive. Chlotar captured Sigebert and his five brothers and summarily executed them. Brunhilda was also taken prisoner. The old queen mother, now nearing seventy, was accused of a catalog of treacheries and royal murders, most of them true. Then she was stripped naked and paraded through the ranks of the soldiers on a camel. At length she was executed by having her arms and legs tied to the tails of wild horses that tore her to shreds as they galloped along dragging her behind. The road where this atrocity was reputedly committed, near Abbeville, is still known in local lore as the *Chausée Brunehaut*, or "road of Brunhilda." Many in Gaul felt the punishment, however horrific, fit the crimes, as one chronicler, an unknown writer given the generic Frankish name *Fredegar*, finished his description of this grisly scene by noting that Chlotar was a *timens Deum*, "one who feared God."

This God-fearing monarch was now not only master of all Gaul, but was keen on having Columbanus come back north and take up residence in his new, Frankish kingdom. He sent a persuasive voice to talk with Columbanus. Eustasius, the current abbot of Luxeuil and thus a beloved figure in the Irishman's eyes, was dispatched to Bobbio. Columbanus appears to have been flattered and pleased, but he did not feel up to crossing the Alps again. It's a curious statement of physical weakness from a man who had only recently reportedly manhandled huge logs. Perhaps Columbanus was indulging in the very excuses he so despised in his own monks, claiming infirmity when he may have actually not wanted to reenter the dangerous swirl of Merovingian politics. Chlotar had shown exceptional vindictiveness toward Brunhilda. Apart from her horrific humiliation and execution he had her body burned and denied a proper Christian burial. Her supporters had later disinterred her remnants and buried them in the monastic settlement of St. Martin's at Autun, a religious foundation she herself had once established. Perhaps Columbanus, who could be difficult and irascible but not bloodthirsty, was loath to dwell in the realm of so brutal a king. He could not have known that Chlotar would rule successfully until he died of natural causes in 629, leaving his kingdom in the capable hands of his son and successor, Dagobert I, one of the greatest kings in Frankish history. Also, it must have been a considerable factor in his thinking that things were going well in Lombardy and a successful conversion of these people to Catholicism seemed imminent.

The crusty, old saint kept his friend and successor Eustasius at Bobbio "for some time" instructing him further in how to be an effective abbot, and finally sent him back north with a letter asking Chlotar to keep the brethren at Luxeuil under royal protection, presumably against the predatory bishops who would devour it. It is to Chlotar's credit that he complied, enriching the monastery and encouraging its growth during the coming years.

Yet as Columbanus entered the final stage of his life he could neither know that his time was near nor that all would remain well. Chlotar might be deposed, given the history of the Merovingians, and the Lombards, while on the cusp of converting, might not do so. The bright light that Columbanus had provided to both society and Church was moving inexorably toward extinction. But as the sun backlights the clouds in a burst of color, there would be one more battle to fight, one more "brightening of the light" as he would phrase it, before the twilight that followed.

Map 9.1 Columbanus in Lombardy

Attacking Arianism

On the surface Columbanus' role in Lombardy seemed straightforward and relatively uncomplicated. The Lombards were near to converting to Trinitarian Catholicism and, while their conversion was no sure thing, there was a clear precedent for it. A quarter century before, in Spain, the Visigothic king Reccared had adopted Catholicism for himself and less than two years later, in 589, had presided over a national church council at Toledo that rejected Arianism for his entire kingdom. This was done in a society that had experienced more Arian-Catholic bitterness than in Lombardy and in a political setting that had, through a bloody rebellion by a royal prince, equated Catholicism with insurrection. If the Visigoths could do it, then surely things looked promising for the Lombards.

Columbanus had gotten right to work on that task. In a series of sermons in Milan, possibly preached in the great cathedral that still bears Ambrose's name, the Irishman had acknowledged his unusual position. Starting his initial sermon with the declaration that "Since I bear the responsibility for very needful teaching, first of all I may briefly speak of the first thing for all to know." And what was that "first thing"? It was salvation, but only for those who believed in the Trinitarian view. As always, Columbanus saw things simply and never resorted to euphemism when a stark description was at hand. The Arian theology was a "poisonous and mad delirium of all the heretics" and its body of literature "a learned irreligion." One can almost see the saint rolling up his sleeves and relishing the opportunity to do battle.

The Basilica of San Ambroglio in Milan. Once the cathedral seat of St. Ambrose, it was here that Columbanus preached his series of sermons in 613, advocating the monastic life and condemning Arianism.

As he had written to his disciples when facing exile, battle was a path to true faith: "If you remove the foe, you remove the battle also; if you remove the battle, you remove the crown as well."

Agilulf had consented to so much, including the invitation to Columbanus, that he seemed only to be asking for a clear explanation of Catholicism that he could accept. But that would prove to be much trickier than expected. Unfortunately for Church unity, at this moment in history there seemed to be two versions of Catholicism from which to choose due to a tangled and unresolved controversy stretching back nearly two centuries. It was not going to be a simple matter of dealing with the Arian heresy alone. Columbanus would have to take sides in this other argument and in so doing successfully negotiate with the Lombard monarchy, the pope, and the accumulated interpretations of theologians living and dead. A man of controversy for his entire sojourn on the continent, Columbanus would find himself in his first real theological battle. His earlier conflicts had mostly been procedural, ranging from matters of hairstyle to the relative autonomy of monasteries. The one real matter of theological importance had been the question of the correct computation of the date for Easter. Even that was, in substance, a procedural and organizational difference. Now the irascible Irishman would have to weigh in on a core belief: the correct interpretation of the very nature and function of Christ.

The Three Chapters Controversy

Here, as in so many other instances, Columbanus showed himself to be Irish and to treasure that heritage at all costs over any recent continental points of view. The Irish had received Christianity during the mid-fifth century at a time when one side of the controversy had not been condemned. Now, more than a century and a half later, Columbanus would uphold what was not only out-of-date, but possibly heretical. His ministry with the Lombards, no matter how impressive his personal behavior and sanctity, would to a large degree depend upon his success in this theological debate. The dispute has come down to us as "The Three Chapters Controversy" because the writings at issue were penned in the fifth century by three Eastern bishops: Theodore of Mopsuestia, Theodoret of Cyrrhus, and Ibas of Edessa. But the matter had more complex origins than that.

As frequently happens in theological disputes, an answer often leads to further questions. So it was when Arianism, the belief that Christ was created after God the Father, was finally put to rest in the late Roman Empire. The decision that God the Father, Son, and Holy Spirit had all existed together from the beginning raised questions about Christ's human status. If He were truly and completely God, then how did He become human? Two schools of thought developed. One, called Nestorianism after its founder Nestorius, the patriarch of Constantinople, held that Christ had two natures, human and divine, but emphasized the human. The other party, led by Cyril, the patriarch of Alexandria, believed Christ had only one nature, the divine. His followers were called monophysites after the Greek words for "one nature" (*mono-physis*). Following a crescendo of controversy, even including some violence, a church council at Chalcedon in 451 finally "solved" the issue. The Emperor Marcian had ordered the assembled bishops to actually read the solution offered by Pope Leo I, the so-called *Tome of Leo*. Up to that point the Eastern bishops had so little respect for Leo's contribution that they used the book to prop up the uneven legs of a table. Now when forced to read and react to it, they accepted Leo's answer, although reluctantly. The solution he proposed was called the hypostatic union and it held that Christ did have two natures, but that they were mysteriously joined so that he was "fully God and fully man."

There the matter more or less rested for more than ninety years. Then the Emperor Justinian decided to reopen the wound by urging the condemnation of three men, now long dead, and their writings. The three men were not of equal standing in the Church's eyes. Theodore of Mopsuestia was considered heretical by most, while Theodoret of Cyrrhus and Ibas of Edessa had been approved by the Council of Chalcedon. The blanket condemnation that Justinian engineered in Constantinople seemed to actually declare the whole of the church council at Chalcedon to be heretical. Needless to say, this played very poorly in the Western Church whose Pope Leo had provided the settlement for the council. One would expect the present Pope Vigilius (r. 537–555) to hurry to the defense of the papacy and oppose Justinian.

But Vigilius had two major problems. He owed his election as pope in large part to the influence of Justinian's wife, the Empress Theodora, so he would be reluctant to battle his benefactor, and his character was not always as resolute under pressure as a leader of Western Christianity should be. Vigilius at first agreed with Justinian, with some vague reservations, then reversed his field only to once again change course and side with the emperor. At one point in this on-again, off-again dispute between the eighty-year-old pope and the emperor concerning the Three Chapters, Justinian ordered Vigilius arrested. When the soldiers came to apprehend him, he clung so desperately to a pillar near the altar in St. Peter's Basilica that he actually pulled it down. Astounded at such resistance from so elderly a man, the troops gave up on taking him into custody and left. All this back and forth only caused division in the Church, and created a problem that would last until the closing years of the seventh century. Vigilius' successor, Pelagius I (p. 556–561), realizing that he had to choose one position or the other, ratified the condemnation of The Three Chapters, but discord and uncertainty persisted. The Church was, in effect, suffering a schism at the very time when the Lombards were looking for unity. The situation was worsened by the minute differences in doctrine within the actual Three Chapters, and the vagueness of Justinian's condemnation. Since the emperor had begun the whole affair in 543 as a way to get lingering Monophysite factions into unity with the rest of his empire, he had, as with compromises in general, made his position loose enough to fit everyone. That only made matters worse. Milan, the old Imperial city, was a hotbed of dissension, so much so that at one point the metropolitan of Milan was forced to live far to the south in Genoa to avoid the attacks of The Three Chapters advocates.

One can almost imagine Columbanus and Theudelinda consulting as to what course of action would be most beneficial. The Irishman had written to Pope Gregory before, on other matters, and Theudelinda was almost a pen pal with that great pontiff. But Gregory was no longer pope, and the congenial relationship of former years may or may not be in force for Pope Boniface IV (r. 608–615), the present occupant of the chair of St. Peter. It was urgent that lines of communication be opened, and quickly. So Columbanus set to work on his longest letter, some 5,000 words, in an effort to heal a wound much larger than Lombardy. He acknowledged this most colorfully and frankly admitting "that the affair is beyond me" and that he felt as if he were "thrusting my face into the fire." But the difficulty of any task never seemed to be a sufficient reason to deter Columbanus from attempting it, and this would be no different.

Since Boniface was not the familiar correspondent with Theudelinda that Gregory once was, Columbanus was careful to frame the letter as coming from Agilulf's request, saying, "When a gentile King of the Lombards asks a dull Scots pilgrim to write … who will not wonder rather than revile?" As always, Columbanus was proud to be Irish. He did not hesitate to point out that "the freedom of his country's customs … has been part-cause of (his) audacity" because the Irish valued a man's principles more than his position. It was a veiled statement that if the pope should err, his authority would no longer be valid—a radically explosive view of papal power. That power, based on Jesus' telling Peter that the apostle would be able to bind and loose things on earth and they would also be bound and loosed in Heaven, was always seen as beyond revocation. The believers, called *laicos*, or "ignorant ones" from which we get the word *layman*, were not to judge whether or not to obey, nor to pick and choose which papal ruling might be legitimate. When Columbanus suggested disobedience if the pope was in error, he expressed a view that, some six or seven centuries later, would be taken up by John Wyclif in England and Jan Hus in Bohemia. Such thinking could lead to reformation, as it did in the sixteenth century. Columbanus' other statements, such as "guilt deprives (them) of the right to judge" when speaking of disagreeable prelates, only underscored this dangerous perspective. While he protested loudly and at length about his absolute fidelity to the papacy—"all are bound to St. Peter's chair"—that fidelity could be lost if the pope lost his orthodoxy "since it was (Peter's) right confession that privileged even the holy bearer of the keys."

The same patterns of speech and almost fanatical bluntness of expression that had characterized Columbanus his whole life appeared here also. He actually seems to lecture Boniface saying "many are doubtful about your faith's integrity," and he reminds Boniface that "you ought to know that your power will be the less in the Lord's eyes, if you even think this (heresy) in your heart." It seems Columbanus had been greeted on his arrival in Lombardy with a letter from a local bishop alleging that the pope was in complete sympathy with the condemnation of The Three Chapters, and the old Irish saint, possibly recalling his profitable use of Theodore of Mopsuestia for the writing of his own biblical commentary, or more probably the blanket condemnation of Chalcedon's rulings, rose up in indignation. But one might wonder why he took such a frontal assault on the issue. Why not tease out of the pope, with appropriately kind words, his true position? Why the unnecessarily confrontational tone? The only answer seems to be that Columbanus' personality, always ready to verbally "thrust his face into the fire," was in full play once more.

Perhaps sensing that he may have gone a bit too far, Columbanus began to soften his words as the letter rolled on. In the end, this "dull" *Scottus*, or Irishman, had a very simple, nontheological solution to that which had tormented minds throughout the Christian world: essentialism. Columbanus wanted the warring parties to focus on their commonly held points and just "refuse to argue over ancient quarrels." Realizing that the question of the nature of Christ was pivotal in the whole of doctrine, he fell back on the point that it was ultimately beyond human understanding; so mysterious that "if any things are doubtful, reserve them for God's judgment." Otherwise, he urged agreement: "For I cannot understand for what reason a Christian can strive about the faith with a Christian." These are the words of a practical man impatient with the delay of argument while the great prize of winning a major nation is slipping away. He closed with just that concern, written ever so bluntly, noting that the Lombards had "long trampled on the Catholic faith … and now they ask that our faith should be confirmed." After mentioning Agilulf twice, once by name, Columbanus did allow Theudelinda into the written plea, saying the royal couple asked that "all should be made one" so that "peace should come quickly to the faith."

Quickly was the operative adverb, as Columbanus, Boniface, and Agilulf were all dead in less than two years. We have no record that the pope responded to Columbanus or that there was further communication. All we know is that, despite living until 628 and assisting her son's reign for at least ten years, Theudelinda was unable to bring the Lombards to Catholicism. More than a century and a half later, the conquests of Charlemagne would enfold the Lombards into what would one day be the Holy Roman Empire and their separate existence and religion would fade. Perhaps the theological dispute was intractable, but one might wonder whether or not certain elements in Rome distrusted this Irish-style monastic church that Columbanus had spread wherever he went. Like the bishops in Gaul, the Roman clergy may have wondered about such a different, and possibly rival, structure taking root in the kingdom of the Lombards, who had attempted in earnest to conquer Rome for generations. If it may be said that Columbanus therefore failed in his last missionary enterprise, it may be said more fairly that it was a failure beyond his control, whether theologically or politically.

At Rest in Bobbio

It was success, rather than failure, that crowned Columbanus' efforts at Bobbio. The infant monastery in the shadow of Mt. Penice grew quickly to preeminence in northern Italy while his other foundations, especially Luxeuil, flourished. Columbanus' biographer, Jonas, is strangely quiet on these last two years of the saint's life. Jonas entered Bobbio in 618, less than three years after Columbanus' death and he became the chief assistant to Attala, one of the old abbot's dear companions. It is hard, given these facts, to believe that Jonas was ignorant of the great man's last years, yet they are largely omitted from the narrative. Perhaps Jonas felt he was writing for the monks of Bobbio and therefore need not record for them things they already knew. The earlier years in Gaul might be unknown to the brothers, but not the last days in Bobbio itself. We can only guess at the omission.

But legend, as always, supplies some "details" for these final days. It was said that as the monks were felling timbers for the ever-growing community of huts, the old Irish boothies that Columbanus knew so well from his early monastic days, a savage bear emerged from the woods and killed one of the oxen used to pull the logs out of the forest. Of course, Columbanus' affinity for bears was brought into play, and the old saint rebuked the beast and yoked it up to finish hauling the logs. It is a remarkable visual picture, a bear teamed with an ox pulling a log wagon, and wholly within the realm of the fantastic. Some historians explain the lack of records and accounts for a given period by claiming that contentment does not require explanation, whereas turmoil does. If so, these must have been golden days at Bobbio.

Having made the commitment not to return to Gaul, now controlled by the friendly monarch Chlotar II, Columbanus was able to do something he had never done before. He preached a series of sermons, probably once again in the Cathedral of St. Ambrose, which did much more than decry Arianism. In effect he was free to recruit, through public appearances, for his monastic movement. Previously his draw had been in personal contact or by hearsay, and often via the working of miracles. Now he was doing the equivalent of advertising to the general public. Despite the theories of marketing, any advertisement ultimately rises or falls on the attractiveness of its product. Columbanus did not soften the hardness of his message in order to attract monastic enrollees. In the follow-up to his anti-Arian sermon, he harped on the critical need for a constant examination of the inner man in order to destroy any sin that might spring up there: "Idle then is a religion decorated with prostrations of the body, equally idle is the mere mortification of the flesh." This type of religion is "hollow devotion" and can be useful only if accompanied by a sincere heart. Here Columbanus was alluding to his scheme of penance that required the believer to examine his own heart daily. Since he had written a penitential for the lay folk as well as for his monks, this sermon was a perfect opportunity to impress on the churchgoing public the need for just such a system. Going through the motions of religion was "as if a field were continually plowed and yet the crop never grew." And the penance Columbanus prescribed for the laity was rough plowing indeed.

The usual approach to this issue is to emphasize the "tariffed" nature of the penance; that sins were ranked according to severity and corresponding punishment prescribed to fit the exact level of transgression. As Columbanus wrote in his penitential, penance must be "in accordance with the greatness of the offenses." While many theologians would argue the point that even smaller sins, those called *peccata minuta*, are just as injurious to the soul as large ones, or *peccata capitalia*, the idea of ranking offenses made perfect sense to the barbarian West. Germanic law codes were based on the idea of bot, or equivalent fines and punishments for equivalent crimes. Knocking out two teeth was often punished twice as severely as the knocking out of one, and an injury to a more essential body part was punished to a greater extent than injury to a lesser one. The application of this general rule to offenses against God, or religion, was seen as an almost logical extension of the regular legal system. It made more sense in a post-Roman context to do this type of penance sin by sin, punishment by punishment rather than to store it all up for one huge, final penance near the end of life. Columbanus addressed this in his penitential: "The diversity of offenses makes a diversity of penances." But he did not see penance as a legal matter, such as the bot system of the Germans. He preferred the metaphor of medicine; penance was a medicinal cure for sick souls. He, and any other abbot, was likened to a doctor administering different medications for different illnesses. "For doctors," he wrote, "compound their medicines in diverse kinds," in order to treat wounds, bruises, boils, fractures, burns, and all manner of sicknesses effectively. So should "spiritual doctors" treat the maladies and mishaps of the soul.

But there was another glaring difference between the "tariffed" penance and the bot system, and this difference was not metaphorical. The law codes of the barbarian West decided the appropriate punishment not only on the degree of the crime but on the status of the participants. Persons of lesser social status, *minores personae*, were held in lower value than nobles, while a free man was more valuable than a slave. Even among slaves, those who were specialists, such as goldsmiths, were worth more than a common field hand. The punishment for a crime was directly related to the relative importance of the victim and the perpetrator. This was certainly not the case with penance. One of the enduring appeals of the Christian religion is the general assumption of equality. All are sinners, so all must do penance, and the penance will be the same for all whether noble or slave. There is no hint of special treatment in

Columbanus' penitential. It is certainly not surprising that this man, bred in a system where Irish nobles deliberately debased themselves in dress, food, housing, and labor, would be no respecter of rank.

So all would be subject to the same vigorous chastisement in order to "cure" sins. The same mind that allowed no excuses for his monks and reveled in a diet of herbs and stale bread while shivering in the scant cover of insufficient shelter would devise a system of penance that was at once quite harsh yet strangely forgiving. Penance involved the following of a strict regimen of denial for a prescribed length of time. Oddly, Columbanus rarely specified exactly what his monks should do for penance; he possibly assumed that other Irish penitential strictures were well known among career monastics. But for the laity, who would find all this fairly novel, he generally spelled out the action as well as the duration required. Columbanus' view of penance was that the punishment be as much as possible a mirror image of the offense. In dealing with his monks, "the talkative is to be punished with silence ... the gluttonous with fasting, the sleepy with watching," and so forth. This general rule was carried over to the laity but with the adjustment that offenses that were minor in secular society, such as talkativeness, would not appear in this scheme. But with both monks and laymen, his objective was that "each suffer exactly in accordance with his desserts, that the just may live justly."

One would expect the harshest penance to be reserved for violent, possibly lethal crimes such as homicide. But in this, Columbanus mimicked much that was barbarian law. According to the early law codes, homicide could be atoned for by the payment of a heavy fine. To be sure, the fine was calculated according to the "value" of the person slain, but it was heavy enough to make the payment of this *wergeld*, or "man-gold," ruinous to the perpetrator and his or her family. This concept was designed to do two things: make killing so expensive that it would not be a feasible option and allow vengeance for the death of a kinsman to be satisfied by a transfer of wealth rather than a resort to a blood feud. Using this point of view, a life would not be required for a life, but a steep outlay of riches would. Columbanus seems to be in touch with this barbarian sentiment here as he prescribes "three years on bread and water as an unarmed exile" for the killer who then, once that is done, will return and render "the due of affection and duty to the relatives of the slain." The three-year sentence also holds for parents who smother their child. The first year will be on bread and water, and the last two years without wine and meats (*vino et carnibus*).

This three years' penance is also prescribed for one who, having committed adultery with another's wife, has produced a child. Here the miscreant will abstain from "the more appetizing foods" as well as from relations with his own wife. After three years he will pay a fine, called *praetium pudicitiae*, or "the price of chastity," to the offended husband and his guilt would be cancelled. The three years' penance with follow-up payments was the strongest penalty in his system, with two exceptions. Only homosexual activity, which required seven years' penance, and deliberate perjury, which required the layman to sell all his property, give it to the poor, and enter a monastery "bidding farewell to the entire world … until death," received a stronger penitential sentence. It may seem odd to us that these offenses ranked higher than murder in this scale of justice. Yet the act of willful perjury, for example, was considered blasphemous in an age where oaths were taken as to God. Apparently the murderer seemed less a threat to the system than one who deliberately mocked divine justice.

A variety of other sexual sins were cataloged as well. Fornication with a widow cost one year, while the same offense with a virgin required two years' penance and a stiff payment. Bestiality was also punished by a year's restriction, as was masturbation. Lust, rather than actual physical sex, was punished by forty days' penance. Theft drew a punishment of 120 days penance and the making of restitution. Habitual theft, however, called for a year and one hundred twenty days as well as giving alms to the poor. Other disruptive behaviors were also punishable. Drunkenness, "to the extent of vomiting," required forty days, as did brawling. In the latter case, if the injuries prevented the victim from working, the offending party was also to "attend to his neighbor's work" until the disabled one was well enough to return to his or her occupation.

Penance was indeed necessary for all, but the constant drumbeat on the issue of purity contained in his sermons suggests that Columbanus knew well that some, if not many, in his audience might go beyond daily penance as a lay-person all the way to entering his monastic foundations. *Purity* is a concept that is total. If striving for it is a good thing for laymen, then why not attempt to reach a higher level of purity as a monk? Of course most of those who heard Columbanus preach did not enter his monastery, but enough did to cause rapid growth. Consequently, he also preached sermons directed particularly to his new monks that elaborated and explained his basic rule that he had established years earlier in Gaul. These are, in many important respects, continuations of his public admonitions in Milan. In *"How the Monk Should Please God,"* he described the successful monk as one who "is mortified in mind sooner than in body." Immodestly calling his system "the training of all training," he later asked the rhetorical question, "Why do you not take notice of yourself, wretched mankind, inwardly rotten … but outwardly a skin washed yet never clean? For you are always stained and defiled from the inner filth of your uncleanness." In an age where most believed that whatever was observed outwardly was a sure guide to inner intent, Columbanus was sounding once again the alarm against hypocrisy. The true Christian, the true monk, would be one whose inner and outer holiness were equally correct.

Having made his case for the monastic life, Columbanus could feel safely and prosperously ensconced in his burgeoning monastery at Bobbio. All seemed well. He could not know that he was nearing his final journey, the one we all must take, from life to death.

In late November 615, as the cold winds whistled around the Apennines, the monks of Bobbio winterized their huts against the inevitable cold. The monastery was still in its infancy, having been founded only a bit more than a year earlier, and did not yet have the extensive buildings and outlands that it would attain in the coming generations. But every indication was encouraging. The ranks of the monastic brothers were swelling and the monastic plant that

Columbanus had lovingly tended was putting down deep roots. No one could foresee that the hand that had cultivated all this growth would soon be stilled.

On Sunday, November 23, Columbanus, saint, pilgrim, monastic pioneer, and nemesis of the proud and overmighty, breathed his last. Legend has it that far away, just off the shores of Lake Constance, Gall, his old friend now estranged, awoke from his sleep to notify his brothers that Columbanus had died. He was informed in one of those prophetic dreams that play around the edges of Columbanus' life from the beginning right up to the end. Feeling certain of the fact, Gall celebrated his first mass in three years as a requiem for his dead mentor. Sudden as the event seems, Columbanus did not simply drop dead, as he had time on his deathbed to send Gall his *cambutta*, or short staff, as a sign of reconciliation for their infamous falling out. The staff arrived in the north much later than the saint's death, seeming to confirm the supernatural origin of Gall's premonition.

Columbanus' Shrine

The death of one acclaimed as a saint is usually the high point in any hagiographic recounting of the subject's life. Once again, the actual date of saints' birth was often considered to be unimportant while their death day, their true "birthday" into heaven, was the key moment. Therefore, most saints lives spend much descriptive time telling of miraculous portents, angel escorts, and the overwhelming impact of the death on colleagues and the faithful, as the saint slips from this life to the next. Yet with Columbanus there is virtually none of that. Scholars have gone to great lengths to explain this absence of detail. Certainly this silence is not because Columbanus was not reckoned a saint.

During his lifetime, he was considered such by common consensus. Even his enemies paid homage to this as they tried to get his approval for their nefarious schemes. Were he not roundly considered to be a saint, such approval would mean little or nothing. Everyone considered him worthy of saintly status, so the silence in the record about his passing cannot originate there.

By far the most popular theory on the lack of detail is that Jonas, having entered Bobbio as a young man only three years after Columbanus' death, knew that his fellow monks were supremely acquainted with all the details and therefore needed no one to recount them. But that supposes that Jonas was writing for a monastic audience exclusively. Most efforts at hagiography, whether initially for a restricted audience such as this or not, were also aimed at posterity. The fact that we still turn to the pages of Jonas' *Vita Sancti Columbani* for instruction on this great man is proof enough that some retelling of the events surrounding his death is necessary whether or not his contemporaries knew it well. Sulpicius Severus' prototypical saint's life, of St. Martin, was penned within a dozen years of the holy man's death—even closer to that event than Jonas' work that was written finally in the early 640s—and contains a full account of Martin's "homegoing." Yet no contemporary account exists of Columbanus' death, nor of its cause.

Once dead, Columbanus was commemorated as was customary for three days, then entombed at Bobbio. He had once written, *viae enim finis nostrae patria nostra est*, "For the end of our road is our home." No doubt he meant that the end of his *peregrinatio* would mean his attainment of heaven. But as with all saints in these formative years of Christianity, where the road ended in death became the burial spot, and thus "home." Often the word *condita*, "founding," was used to describe the saint's resting place; it was the exact word used by Romans to describe the founding of their city. Much like a city, the saint was founded or established in the spot where he or she lay entombed. In an era that melded nature and supernature, the saint was considered to be fully in the hand of God, and thus able to advocate for the faithful with Christ, and also fully present in the tomb, in order to be accessible to those who would come for healing, resolution, or the like. As always, St. Martin's saint cult offers an instructive model. Over his tomb at Tours was the following inscription: *Hic conditus est sanctae memoriae Martinus episcopus, cuiius anima in manu Dei est, sed hic totus est, praesens manifestus omni gratiam virtutum* (as Peter Brown has translated it: "Here lies Martin the bishop, of holy memory, whose soul is in the hand of God; but he is fully here, present and made plain in miracles of every kind"). For the believers who streamed there the saint's tomb was a reliable point of contact between the healing holiness of heaven and the multiple needs of earth.

Consequently, there was often serious dispute between locales over who should get the privilege, and pilgrimage revenue, of having the saint's tomb. Once again the plight of St. Martin of Tours offers an instructive example. Martin, who was bishop of Tours for nearly a quarter century, had the

Columbanus' tomb at Bobbio. It was only after the monastery there modified its Irish customs and allowed the general public to visit the saint's tomb that Columbanus began to attain the status of other notable saints.

misfortune to die while on a pastoral visit to the little Loire River town of Candes. The local townsfolk were overjoyed that the great man had expired in their little hamlet and confidently expected growth in wealth and significance due to their possession of Martin's tomb. The citizens of Tours were chagrined; he was their bishop after all, and made haste to correct the situation. As the people of Candes were honoring Martin for the requisite three days, the men of Tours glided their boats down the Loire under cover of night and stole Martin's body. Quickly bringing it to Tours, they buried the saint on November 11, 397. Once buried, he was theirs, and even to the present St. Martin's Day is held to be November 11 rather than his actual death day of November 8. It could get nasty when saintly remains were involved.

There appears to be no such nastiness surrounding Columbanus' burial, or "founding" at Bobbio in spite of the fact that his monasteries at Annegray and Luxeuil might make a better claim to their patron's body. Even though the tendency was to keep saints buried in the place of their original interment, it was possible for them to be moved. The term for this was *translation*, and it could be applied to a saint's body that had newly been discovered and then moved to a place of honor or it could also be applied to saintly bodies moved out of necessity. The Abbey of St. Wandrille in France, for example, was attacked so frequently by Vikings during the ninth century that the monks were obliged to dig up St. Wandrille's remains and relocate them several times. But generally the burial of a saint was final. There was also the option of multiple burials of various body parts as a way of establishing a saint in all the places he or she founded, but the central resting place retained primacy. The problem with the partitioning of the saint's remains, of course, was that there was only so much of any given body to go around. A more unlimited way to accomplish this was to use contact relics rather than actual portions of the saint. A contact relic was anything that touched the saint or saintly tomb. It could even be something in near proximity to the tomb such as dust from the ground or oil from the ubiquitous hanging lamps of the tomb's chamber.

But the appeal of these saintly "branch offices" could never be as great as the central resting place of the saint. Pilgrims would flock to the main shrines seeking cures for physical, emotional, or spiritual maladies or to render thanks for remedies already received. The belief that the saint was both "fully here" and fully in heaven advocating for believers made the shrine a *locus sanctorum*, or "holy place." Saint's tombs exercised such social and religious power that the invading Muslim armies under Abderrahman, surging up through southern France in 732, had as their objective the conquest and destruction of the Basilica of St. Martin at Tours and its saintly sarcophagus. Their intention was to demoralize Christian resistance by taking the single most popular saintly shrine in the West of that day. As a result of their target selection, the Muslims were defeated just short of their objective, between the cities of Tours and Poitiers, in a fierce battle with the Frankish commander, Charles, forever after known as *Martel*, or "the Hammer." A popular saint's shrine could be the virtual nerve center of society and often included the necessary accompaniment of businesses such as inns, eateries, and even merchandisers of holy relics, such as vials of oil from the lamps around the tomb, or bits of cloth that had touched the sarcophagus. In some ways, these zones of development replaced the bustling commercial sectors of the old Roman towns, now largely emptied, or shrunken, in the confused and dangerous aftermath of the fall of the empire.

Consequently, the number of miracles worked at the saint's tomb far outstripped the miracles actually done by the saint while alive. This was necessary in that pilgrims would not continue to stream to a shrine that was unproductive. St. Martin became the preeminent saint in Gaul during this period by just such means. While his original life story became the prototypical saint's hagiography, the accumulated miracles at his tomb, growing in number annually, eventually required additional volumes detailing and explaining this phenomenon. Thus, Bishop Gregory of Tours, famed as a historian of sixth century Gaul but also the custodian of the saint's tomb and cult, felt compelled to write a multipart work called *De Virtutibus Sancti Martini*, or "On the Holy Deeds of Saint Martin." *Virtus*, a word that looks much like our modern word *virtue*, did not mean Martin was a virtuous man, although he was, but meant "holy deeds," or the good things God was able to do through his saint. These holy deeds were by nature miraculous. So the books Gregory wrote described the continual flow of miracles from God through Martin and his tomb to the faithful who came for assistance there.

Recent scholarship has identified the code words that indicated whether or not a person subscribed to this belief in saintly power. Those who believed in the saints' abilities to access heaven were said to have *reverentia*, or "reverence." Those who did not believe were said to have *temeritas*, or "temerity," the rash audacity of unbelief. Sometimes the old prevalence of pagan ideas in the countryside, or *pagus*, would encourage writers to describe nonbelievers in saintly power as having *rusticitas*, or "rusticity." At any rate, the world of Columbanus was apparently one in which society was divided between reverent believers in the saints and "rash" nonbelievers. For those who believed, however, there was great power at these holy tombs.

According to the beliefs of the saint cults of the period, this power was not available everywhere. Since a saint's power and holiness were located where he or she actually was buried, this posed a serious limiting factor on his or her miraculous reach. This may explain the popularity of establishing outposts of the saint's presence in other locations. A little bit of the saint, or a sufficiently impressive contact relic, could assign an oratory, monastery, or parish church to the control of the contributing holy person. It resembled a form of religious extraterritoriality, where an originating saint could have lands and churches far distant from the home foundation under his or her purview. While these outposts were not as certain a contact point with heaven as the home base, they were just as authentically under the saint's control. That's why one can find churches dedicated to Gallic saints, such as the ubiquitous Martin, in England, Spain, or Italy. It also explains why armies on the march, or even travelers making their way cross country, felt constrained to pray to the appropriate saint of the territories they passed through. A famous example of this was the Frankish king Clovis' march south from northern

Gaul to battle the Visigoths in 507. When informed that his men had stolen fodder from fields under the protection of St. Martin, he punished the offending troops and was said to have exclaimed, "Where will our hope of victory be if we offend the blessed Martin?"

It was only in the later Middle Ages that the emphasis shifted from the saints' territorial control to an emphasis on their function. By the later centuries most of the lands and churches had been already assigned, so it became a more prevalent practice to view a saint as having power not just in a specific place but in a situation that corresponded to his or her life and experiences. Therefore, St. Christopher was the saint one appealed to for traveling mercies since he legendarily carried Christ across a stream. St. Denis, who would eventually replace St. Martin as the main saint of France, was said to be good for headaches since he was beheaded during the persecutions of the early 300s. One appealed to the appropriate saint based on a connection between what the saint had experienced and the crisis that the faithful was currently encountering.

This could have almost humorous application. Frequently saints were assigned helpful functions based on the sound of their names rather than their actual experiences. Thus St. Roche was deemed to be helpful against pestilence, St. Clarus for vision problems, St. Lupus for protection against wolf attack, and in the most egregious example, the hosiers guild in Paris chose St. Sebastian as their patron saint because his name sounded like the early French phrase for "his socks hold up" (se bas ses tiennent). But in the world of Columbanus, the issue was not largely one of function but territory. In this age, the saint would be entombed in a specific place that would serve as the command center for a growing network of territorial control. The flow of public petitioners and their miraculous resolutions of their problems at the tomb site would only magnify the holy one's power and ensure continued territorial reach. Oddly, this was not what happened at Bobbio, nor was it largely the fate of the Columbanus' legacy.

Even though Columbanus was interred at Bobbio, he is not known as "St. Columbanus of Bobbio." While there are many little towns named some version of Columbanus, for example, San Colombo, and Sainte-Colombe, there is not the territorial fixation normally seen in late Antique or early Medieval saint cults. He is not St. Columbanus of Luxeuil, Bobbio, or any particular place and his whole cult seems unattached to the "saintly territorialism" of the period. This can be read, as other biographers of Columbanus have done, as signifying his status as the "first European." He was, they would argue, not assigned to a particular location because of his cosmopolitan career. His wide-ranging and generalized geographical presence as well as his variegated cultural contacts made him impossible to confine to one home area.

In spite of this theory, there still remains a touch of mystery as to why he was not the subject of such territorialism. One can conjecture that his view of life as a continual journey would naturally weaken any attachment to a certain location. For a man who was constantly on the move, and, like saints customarily do, who considered the ultimate destination of his lifelong journeys to be heaven, the exact resting place of the body would not be that significant.

But what Columbanus thought was not the deciding factor. Saints' tombs existed as access points to the supernatural in the minds of believers and not in the expressed attitudes of the deceased saint. Whether or not Columbanus wanted to be "founded" would not decide the popularity of his tomb site. If the same public who had deemed him to be a saint in the first place also believed him to be specially located in power at Bobbio, then that would be the case. There was a certain degree of public opinion associated with the holy in these situations. But once again, there seems to be very little evidence for the type of development in Columbanus' cult and the tomb itself that one might find in other well-known saints such as St. Martin or St. Julian of Brioude.

Columbanus' tomb does not seem to be an acclaimed public point of holy power accompanied by so many petitioners that volumes would be required to catalog the sheer numbers of miracles. Given Columbanus' eagerness to convert the Lombards, it would certainly make sense if this were so. The petitioners could be seen as representing a postmortem piece of missionary work. Columbanus' tomb, open to all, perhaps could have put the finishing touches on the conversion of the Lombard populace away from Arianism to orthodox Catholicism. Decades before, during the reign of Alboin, the founding conqueror of Lombardy, Bishop Nicetius of Trier had written daring him to assess the competing religions' validity by comparing the miracles performed at their respective saints' shrines. After cataloging an impressive list of healings and exorcisms occurring at Catholic sites, he taunted the king: "Does this happen in the churches of the Arians?" Then, not waiting for an argumentative reply, he concluded, "By no means; for God and the lords the saints are not sensed to be present there." Columbanus' holy presence at Bobbio with the accompanying complement of miracles might well have done as much, if not more, to move the Lombards to Catholicism as his fiery sermons preached while alive.

So why was there a relative lack of clientele at his tomb? Here the culprit might be the Irish characteristics of the Bobbio monastery itself. Typically, a saint's tomb would be in the basement of a church and thus open to all. The only issue involved the need for the *ostiarius*, or keeper of the church keys, to unlock the church so that petitioners could have access to the tomb. The prevalence of holy theft, where some would steal the saint's relics, portions of the sarcophagus, the contact relics such as the lamps and their oil, or even dust from around the tomb, made it necessary for parts of the church to be locked. But in Columbanus' case, his tomb would be located in the interior church of an Irish monastery, and the interior part was a *clausura*, or restricted area. The same constraints that kept Merovingian kings from entering the holiest parts of the Columbanian monasteries would also limit easy access for the petitioning public. Some would qualify for an audience at the tomb and some would commemorate Columbanus in the scattered locations dedicated to him, but the apparatus for his attaining and maintaining ranking status as a major Western saint was largely lacking.

It was only in the tenth century, more than three centuries after the saint's death, that his tomb reached the status of a public shrine. Toward the end of that century an unknown monk at Bobbio penned *De Virtutibus Sancti Columbani,* a mirror of the now standard work chronicling miracles at saints' tombs. This may have been prompted by the events of July 929, when the local magnate, Hugh of Provence, ordered Columbanus' remains to be taken from their resting place and paraded in Pavia to quell an uprising by rebellious nobles. The intention was that "if they would see that holiest body brought there for the sake of his goods, they would stop their robberies." After their return, and reburial at Bobbio, Columbanus' remains "performed many miracles." But the infrequent showing of the saint's body followed by its reinterment at Bobbio would not permit the general public access to his shrine. It may be that as the decades passed and the "Irish" monastery of Bobbio became more and more a mainstream Catholic one, the old Celtic prohibition of unauthorized visitors to the clausura wore away allowing admittance to the tomb for all.

Whatever the reason, Columbanus, recognized by all on the continent as a saint, would repose for the centuries as one who did not produce a growing body of miracle literature or an extensive network of associated territorial relic sites. Yet despite these seeming limitations, he would leave an impressive legacy that reproduced itself in succeeding generations.

11

The Legacy

If Columbanus' cult did not become a continual and growing presence in the Europe of succeeding centuries, and if his efforts to convert the pagans around Lake Constance as well as lure the Lombards away from Arianism were largely failures, what can one claim for his legacy? He did survive the hostility of high-ranking churchmen and violent royals for more than a decade of intense confrontation, no mean feat in itself. But others—here one thinks of the slightly earlier career of Gregory of Tours—have accomplished that. He also set off a wave of Irish pilgrims to the continent so much so that eventually the Gallic churchmen felt it necessary to meet in councils at Soissons (744), and Tours (813), to ban *episcopi et sacerdotes vagrantes*, "wandering bishops and clerics." While these measures were undoubtedly aimed at vagrant ecclesiastics of any ethnicity, their primary instigation seemed to be the large, unaccountable Irish presence.

A Growing Monastic Network

Columbanus did personally found four monasteries that grew in influence as they progressed through the years. But having done that, what separates him from several others equally distinguished? While this is a singular accomplishment, it does not earn for him a special niche in the annals of European history. In terms of Columbanus' contribution to the spread of Western monasticism it would be his secondary impact that would secure his legacy.

It is an often-emphasized fact that within two generations of his death, there were at least ninety-four monasteries in existence that owed their foundations to either Columbanus or his disciples and converts. When discussing these sites, preeminence is generally reserved for the four monasteries that Columbanus founded himself: Annegray, Luxeuil, Fontaines, and Bobbio, although only Luxeuil and Bobbio would have enduring significance. But this Irish *peregrinus* seemed to spin off monasteries as he traveled back and forth through Gaul and eventually from the Rhine to Lombardy. Those companions whose resolution did not measure up to these arduous journeys often dropped out and founded their own Columbanian abbeys, therefore leaving a bit of this Irish system along the way.

A representative sampling of this phenomenon would certainly include the celebrated dispute with Gall and his subsequent founding of a monastery in the Arbon Forest that would one day bear his name: St. Gallen. Traumatic and dramatic as this split between the master and his beloved companion was, it was by no means the only time a brother left the group to establish his own community. Earlier, as the Irish members of Columbanus' band were on their exile journey toward Nantes, one Deicola, possibly a Latinized form of the Irish name *Dicuil*, became so fatigued by the trek that he could go no farther. Apparently Columbanus was not suspicious of his physical weakness as he was with Gall at Lake Constance, perhaps because Deicola was reportedly quite elderly. The aging monk set up camp as a solitary in the woods, but soon so impressed the locals with his sanctity that he found himself the de facto abbot of a monastic settlement. It became known as the Abbey of Lure and was organized on the same Columbanian lines that Deicola had experienced in his career.

On that same exile trip, a monk named *Potentius* also begged off the journey and founded a monastery, now lost, near Coutances. Once again no mention is made of any hard feelings between this man and Columbanus. Later, when Columbanus and his brothers left Bregenz bound for Lombardy, Ursicinus stayed behind as they passed near modern-day Berne, Switzerland, and set up a monastic house later called Saint Ursanne in his honor. Another fellow traveler, with the Frankish name *Sigebert*, split off on this same trip to found an abbey in "Desertina," an apparent reference to the Columbanian habit of seeking deserted places as monastic sites. This particular establishment became the Abbey of Disentis. It seems as if in Columbanus' travels he broadcast monastic seeds wherever he went. The Columbanian nature of these derivative monasteries is complete even to the hagiographic miracle stories that accompany their foundations. So it was that Gall, in true Columbanian fashion, was said to have commanded a bear to throw logs on a fire as he organized his settlement and Deicola healed the nearly severed finger of a worker with his saliva just as Columbanus was said to have done years before for his monastic brother, Theudegisel.

But it was not only monks in Columbanus' system who founded monasteries. He seemed to inspire people outside the religious life to dedicate their children to a "renunciation of the world." These youngsters would go on to establish communities in the Columbanian model that would further furnish the European landscape with Irish-style monasticism. When Columbanus stayed at Vulciacum, the estate of a nobleman named *Authari*, the lady of the house, Aiga, brought her three little sons to him to be blessed. Apparently two of these boys made good on their childhood commissioning as Ado became a monk and founded the Abbey of Jouarre, while his brother Dado, also known as Audoenus or Ouen, entered the monastic life as well and founded the Abbey of Rebais.

When Columbanus intervened miraculously for the Frankish Duke Wandelen and his Roman wife Flavia that they might have children, the boy born to them, called Donatus or "gift," grew up to found a Columbanian-style monastery at Palatium and write a rule for nuns based on Columbanus' monastic regulations.

His mother Flavia busied herself in her widowhood by founding a convent and his brother Chramnelen, apparently joining in the family passion, founded his own Columbanian monastery as well.

By far the most famous story of this kind involves the family of a Frankish noble named *Chagneric* who escorted Columbanus on his trip from his would-be exile at Nantes to Metz and the Austrasian court. During Columbanus' stay at Chagneric's estate, the family became so taken by the Irish holy man that their son and daughter, Faron and Burgundofara, were drawn to the monastic life. Although the balky Chagneric later attempted to talk the daughter out of her commitment, she prevailed and was credited with founding the famous convent of Evoriacum, later called Faremoutiers. Faron took a slightly different path and became bishop of Meaux.

It would be tedious to list all the monasteries founded in the wake of Columbanus' wide-ranging career. Some vanished or diminished in succeeding generations, but the roster includes many that would play large roles in the European church for centuries to come. Columbanus must be seen as a great generator of the monastic impulse that coursed through the continent in this era.

Influences on the Church

Ironically, Columbanus left his mark on the episcopate as well. His long-time nemeses, the Gallic bishops, would find their numbers increasingly filled by disciples of their Irish opponent. Besides the aforementioned Faron, who became bishop of Meaux, Dado (Audoen) not only founded the monastery of Rebais but became bishop of Rouen as well. Within the same fifty-year time span following Columbanus' death that saw a burst of monastic foundations in his name, Columbanian churchmen became bishops at Thérouanne, Vermandois, Noyon, Laon, and Verdun. In an almost dialectical fashion, the old antitheses of Columbanus and the Gallic bishops blended into a new synthesis for the Church. How this actually happened is problematical, but in this period the consensus of the people and the approval of neighboring bishops could secure an Episcopal appointment. By what appears to be a form of popular osmosis, those who subscribed to Columbanus' view on religion began to pervade significant portions of the Gallic Church hierarchy.

This apparently had an effect on easing monastic-Episcopal antipathies as well, for it appears that the Irish independence so on display in Columbanus' own monasteries eventually eroded Episcopal control. The most flagrant examples were Luxeuil, which was under the protective wing of Chlotar II and his successor Dagobert I (r. 629–639), and Bobbio, which secured a papal exemption from Episcopal control in 628.

But the blending did not stop with monastic-Episcopal relations. A development of more consequence for the Western Church may be best exemplified by an inscription that appeared within the first century of the saint's death over the entrance to Columbanus' tomb at Bobbio, calling him a "disciple of Benedict." Given the supposed antagonistic relationship between the Celtic and Benedictine forms of monasticism as experienced in the British Isles during the mid- and late seventh century, it is nothing short of amazing to see Columbanus, as Celtic as possible in his monastic outlook, called a Benedictine right at his tomb. Yet it is a measure of the difficulty in categorizing the lasting impact of this outspoken man that his Episcopal enemies seem to have been won to his side even as the monastic alternative, the Benedictine system, seems to have absorbed him into his structure. It appears that Columbanian monasteries frequently used the *Rule of St. Benedict* as well as that of their founder's in regular practice. So common was this fusion that within three generations Columbanus could be seen plausibly to be "Benedictine." Modern scholarship has done much to illuminate this surprising compatibility between supposedly rival systems. Since the contemporary evidence betrays no hostility between the two on the continent, the assumption of conflict may be just that, an assumption only. Pierre Riché concludes his analysis of the growth of monasticism in this era by noting that "a Columban monastery was no different organizationally from any other." Here he was referring to the disciplinary measures and liturgy rather than the peculiar Irish touches such as the *clausura* and the *vallum*. T. M. Charles-Edwards, noting the existence of a "mixed rule" in Columbanian monasteries, sees no "clash of principles" between the two monastic models.

These conclusions answer retrospectively the old question perplexing students of Columbanus: Why did the Benedictine Rule appear in Columbanian monasteries? The answers they constructed ranged from the supposedly milder outlook of Benedict's regulations to a type of personality cult in Columbanus' monasteries that depended too heavily on the saint himself and thus was somewhat adrift and vulnerable to outside influence with his passing. Some have even detected *lacunae*, or "gaps," in the Columbanian rule that could be filled only by a resort to a complementary Benedictine source. All these hypotheses depend to some degree on there being an adversarial, or at least competitive, relationship between the views of Columbanus and Benedict. If no such relationship existed, however, the blending of the two types falls more naturally within the realm of the probable. Benedictine monasticism may not have "conquered" Columbanian foundations, but rather have been voluntarily sought. Rather than invasion, it may be a matter of invitation.

If that is so, and the facts of this blending are far more certain than the motivations for it, Columbanus has a role to play in one of the most decisive developments in Western culture. Benedict's monastic system has roundly, and rightly, been credited with altering the old Roman views on work and progress. The ancient perspective, that work was a sentence to be ended or avoided if possible, or at best a necessary evil, was replaced by Benedict's view that stated *laborare est orare*, "to work is to pray." This sanctification of labor defeated the old *aurea mediocritas*, or "golden mean," approach that advocated working only until one amassed enough worldly wealth to quit. If labor actually were "worship," it could never really be done enough. This viewpoint was also a powerful antidote to the Eastern-style monastic view that labor generally was to be avoided as catering to the evil material world. The popularization of the Benedictine attitude to labor created a work ethic that would drive European society forward.

But how did these radical changes spread throughout Europe? The election of Gregory the Great, a Benedictine monk, as pope in 590 is correctly seen as a major turning point in this process. But given the fact that Columbanus influenced so many monasteries in his day and encouraged, or at least accepted, the use of Benedict's rule alongside his own, the Irishman may be credited, as Charles-Edwards has said, as "the most important promoter of the Benedictine Rule before Charlemagne and Louis the Pious." Columbanus then may have served as a conduit through which the valuable perspectives of Benedict traveled north into the further reaches of the continent.

This successful melding of the two may have spelled trouble for Celtic monasticism as a whole. As a "mixed rule" enjoyed success, differences between Celtic and Benedictine approaches, such as tonsures and the calculation of Easter, would be highlighted as annoyances, or perhaps impediments to unity, rather than genuine varieties of practice. Had the Celtic monastic system that Columbanus implanted on the continent remained wholly apart from the Romano-Benedictine form, perhaps the Celtic style might have been in a stronger position. Partial accommodation may have encouraged complete absorption, especially when unity was the desired goal of the Church hierarchy.

Cultural and Political Influences

This "mixed rule," existing as a blending of Irish and Roman cultures, was abetted and enlarged by the Germanic presence in Columbanus' monasteries. Germanic culture is inscribed in the rosters of Columbanian monks both during and after his life. The egalitarianism of the monks, who came from various cultures and various stations in life, reduced differences interculturally. The popularity of Columbanus' monasteries among barbarian and Roman, as well as the occasional transient Irish, creates a blending process with the monastery serving as the point of mixture. The Irish penitentials, organized on a basis so familiar to the Germanic law codes, yet written in Latin, are one example of the common touchstone and cultural intersection that Columbanian monasteries provided. The Germanic law perspective that assigned appropriate punishments for crimes, the bot system, was mirrored in the penitential listings of Columbanus. As Edward James has pointed out, "Ireland was the first territory outside the Latin-speaking world in the West to receive Christianity," and it was this affinity with "people like them" that may have been the primary draw of the barbarians to the Irish monasteries. The interplay between barbarian and Roman was already a story several centuries old, but this fresh voice from a land where, like the Germans, Latin and literacy were acquired, not native, tools created a common religious ground that they could all share. Columbanus' monasteries reinterpreted civilization in such a way that a European, rather than an Irish, Germanic, or Latin, product was created. He may not be "the first European," as his too ardent admirers have asserted, but his career facilitated the creation of such a concept. That creative blending could produce an influential result. A French monk at Bobbio, with the Frankish name *Gerbert*, rose to become the abbot there and later attained the papacy as Pope Sylvester II (p. 999–1003). He has been widely credited with lifting the intellectual level of Europe by encouraging the preservation of ancient manuscripts.

Columbanus left more than the wood and stone of monastic houses, and more than the intramural regulations of sequestered monks as a legacy. He left conceptual changes that would alter European civilization in ways and places far from the monastery. An overlooked impact of Columbanus' popularizing of the Irish tariffed penance is that of its effect on the political landscape of Europe. The old, public form of penance was not only a problem for the average believer but could have serious national consequences as well. Since one of the disqualified activities after receiving penance was governmental rule, a count, a duke, or even a monarch could be prohibited from resuming governance after doing penance. As long as the rites were done at the very end of life, there would be no problem. But if the penitent were to survive, so too would the disqualification.

Visigothic Spain provides the clearest example of this dilemma. In October 680, King Wamba, who like most later Visigothic monarchs attained the throne under contentious circumstances, fell deathly ill. Wamba was "quite elderly" when he ascended the throne in 672, so he might be forgiven for believing his days to be at an end. The king was given the penitential discipline of the old style, still in force in the Spain of that day, dressed in a monastic habit and tonsured. But the deathwatch proved to be in vain. Wamba recovered from his illness and sought to resume his rule. Since he was under penance, he was barred from doing so and was forced off the throne. This was not without precedent as the previous monarch, Chindaswinth, had forced penance on his predecessor as a way of guaranteeing his disqualification to rule. Wamba was permitted to nominate his successor, but the old ex-king died three years later, never having regained his power. The events surrounding his deposition contributed to growing instability in late Visigothic rule—an instability that made the kingdom an inviting target for future Muslim invaders.

The spread of the Irish system of daily, private penance that did not disqualify the penitent from former pursuits would allow monarchs, as well as lesser governmental rulers, to retain their authority after making atonement for transgressions. It is hard to imagine, for example, the English King Henry II (r. 1154–1189), being deposed in the aftermath of the killing of the Archbishop of Canterbury, Thomas Becket, in late December 1170, yet that would be a real possibility under the old system of penance. As it was, Henry did a public penance in sackcloth and ashes for his complicity in the murder and reigned for nearly twenty years more. The turning point that this adjustment in penitential theory represented had profound effect on the future governmental development of Europe. The role of Columbanus in this redirection of history should not be overlooked or underestimated. While we might agree with the assessment of J. H. Hexter that historians should doubt the paternity of an event born so long after its parent, it is hard to feature the history of medieval government without factoring in the precondition of penitential change that Columbanus championed.

An additional line of development coming out of Columbanus' spread of the Irish penitential system was its impact on the association of warfare and religion. Old-style penance forbade the penitent to ever again take up arms; a prohibition that would, if all who were required did the necessary penance, decimate the manpower pool for the military. Consequently, this particular limitation of old-style penance was one more factor in encouraging the delay of the rite until the penultimate moment of life. With the daily, tariffed penance of the Irish the resumption of military service was not forbidden, once the penance was complete. Kings could field armies containing soldiers who had done, if the theory actually became practice, penance many times. It was not allowed, however, for one actually in the process of the penitential act to fight.

How does this impact the civilization of Europe beyond providing sufficient manpower for military recruitment? More than four and one half centuries after Columbanus' death the world was treated to the spectacle of armed pilgrims, actually using the old term *peregrini* to describe their status, fighting to reconquer the Holy Land in the First Crusade. The journey from a prohibition against penitents ever fighting again to penitents using warfare as a form of penance began, in some ways, with Columbanus and his Irish model. The initial step of permitting a penitent to resume activity as a warrior needed, of course, to be further developed by the linkage of pilgrimage to penance as well as the eleventh-century papal decision that permitted a pilgrim to bear arms. But the penitential nature of the Crusader armies, often rightly ascribed to successive rulings by a series of ninth-century popes, Leo IV, John VIII, and Nicholas I, has as one of its enabling preconditions that penance does not disqualify military participation. Columbanus, who frowned on war, could not have known the potential military uses in which his daily penance would one day be employed.

But that is a statement that could apply to most of Columbanus' legacy. While we cannot be absolutely certain, owing to the paucity of material about his intentions, we might assume that Columbanus did not set out to direct Western thought on politics, warfare, or even the organization of the Church as a whole. He seems to have been interested in solitude for himself and his brother companions and, whenever brought by the course of events into a position of influence with the public, to advocate for "the still severer precept" of intense religious revival. But the confrontational tone of his message as well as his blunt delivery made it unavoidable that he engage larger issues. In so doing, he set in motion changes that long outlived him, and outlived his memory as well. His impact appears to have been submerged in the larger flow of events leading to a general neglect of his role. Perhaps he had a foreboding of this when he wrote a poem to a monastic brother named *Sethus*. Finishing the lines, Columbanus closed with "a humble prayer" that the reader would be "mindful of me when you read these verses." We too should be mindful of this impetuous, charismatic, and contentious figure as we read the "verses" of European history and consider the ways he gave them form and meaning.

A Note on the Sources

A n excellent place to begin a study of Columbanus is to turn to his own considerable body of writing. The best edition is that of G. S. M. Walker, ed. *Sancti Columbani: Opera* (Dublin: The Dublin Institute for Advanced Studies, 1957). He uses the English text opposite the Latin to make the work available to the general public. Walker includes some writings, parts of the letters and sermons, and many of the poems, which have been the subject of debate as to Columbanus' authorship. For these critiques, see J. W. Smit, *Studies on the Language and Style of Columba the Younger* (Amsterdam: Adolf M. Hakkert, 1971). Ludwig Bieler's work, *The Irish Penitentials* (Dublin: The Dublin Institute for Advanced Studies, 1963), also reproduces Columbanus' penitentials with Latin and English on alternate pages as well as helpful commentary on the text.

Jonas of Bobbio's life of Columbanus is still to be found in the old translation by Dana Carleton Munro, *The Life of St. Columban by the Monk Jonas* (Philadelphia: University of Pennsylvania, 1895). The Latin text, *Ione Vitae Sanctorum Columbani*, is in the *Monumenta Germaniae Historica, S.S. rerum Merovingicarum*, iv, edited by Bruno Krusch (Hannover: Hahn, 1902). The tenth-century *Miracula Sancti Columbani*, detailing his enduring legacy, is found in the *Monumenta Germaniae Historica,* S.S. xxx, pt. 2 edited by H. Bresslau (Hannover: Lipsiae, 1932).

Histories from the lands and age in which Columbanus worked are also quite important for supplying interpretive context. Chief among these would have to be Gregory of Tours' *Libri Historiarum Decem*, which covers the history of Gaul up to the year Columbanus arrived there. It is found in Lewis Thorpe, trans. *Gregory of Tours: History of the Franks* (Harmondsworth: Penguin, 1974). Other histories of the Frankish Gaul of Columbanus' day are J. M. Wallace-Hadrill, trans. *The Chronicon of Fredegar and Its Continuators* (London: Thomas Nelson, 1960), and Bernard S. Bachrach, trans. *Liber Historiae Francorum* (Lawrence, KS: Coronado Press, 1973). The former was written by an anonymous author, or authors, and was simply assigned a typical Frankish name during the Middle Ages, while the latter contains a brief, but fanciful, collection of stories about the demise of Theudebert and Theuderic in 612/613. For the Lombard material, the best source is that of William Dudley Foulke, trans. *History of the Lombards by Paul the Deacon* (Philadelphia: University of Pennsylvania Press, 1907, rpt.

1974). The Germanic law codes provide insight into the culture and particularly into their view on punishment. Katherine Fischer Drew has done excellent work on those nations most connected to Columbanus in her translations of *The Burgundian Code* (Philadelphia: University of Pennsylvania Press, 1972) and *The Lombard Laws* (Philadelphia: University of Pennsylvania Press, 1973).

Secondary works are headed up by the various biographies in English of Columbanus. These have appeared sporadically, every decade or so, over the last century. An excellent older work is that of Helena Concannon, *The Life of St. Columban: A Study of Ancient Irish Monastic Life* (Dublin: Catholic Truth Society of Ireland, 1915). This work, while very dated in interpretation, still contains legendary details not readily found elsewhere that add dimension and flavor to the Columbanian story. Marguerite Marie DuBois' *Un pionnier de la civilisation occidentale: Saint Colomban* (Paris, 1950) is a brief (less than 100 pages of text) account of the saint that was esteemed highly enough to be translated into an English edition by James O'Carroll as *Saint Columban: A Pioneer of Western Civilization* (Dublin: M. H. Gill and Son, 1961). Francis MacManus' *Saint Columban* (New York: Sheed and Ward, 1962) and Tomás Ó Fiaich's *Columbanus in His Own Words* (Dublin: Veritas Publications, 1974) are helpful: the former for its poetic writing and the latter for its commentary on Columbanus' writings as well as the "tour guide" quality of its analysis of his travels. Columbanus shares the limelight in two other works of the 1960s. Eleanor Shipley Duckett's fine book *The Gateway to the Middle Ages: Monasticism* (Ann Arbor: University of Michigan Press, 1961) contains much material on Columbanus, while Brendan LeHane's *The Quest of Three Abbots* (New York: Viking Press, 1968) features him as one of its three eponymous subjects. The most recent biography of Columbanus is that of Katherine Lack, *The Eagle and the Dove: The Spirituality of the Celtic Saint Columbanus* (London: Triangle/SPCK, 2000). While it does what it sets out to do, examine the spiritual side of Columbanus and his career, it does not place him in the necessary historical context.

Contemporary scholarship on the various facets of Columbanus' world includes T. M. Charles-Edwards' fine study *Early Christian Ireland* (Cambridge: Cambridge University Press, 2000) that gives quite a bit of information and interpretation on Columbanus, as well as the Irish religious milieu that was his background. Daíbhí Ó Cróinín's *Early Medieval Ireland, 400–1200* (London: Longman, 1995) is an excellent work that rises well above the genre of a general history of the period. Also valuable is the collection of essays in Michael Lapidge, ed. *Columbanus: Studies on the Latin Writings* (Woodbridge: Boydell Press, 1997). Especially helpful in this latter work are the articles by David Bullough on "The Career of Columbanus" (pp. 1–28) and Charles-Edwards' examination of "The Penitentials of Columbanus" (pp. 217–239). Lisa M. Bitel's *The Isle of the Saints: Monastic Settlement and Christian Community in Early Ireland* (Ithaca: Cornell University Press, 1993) is a well-written compendium of details on the Irish monastic structure and is particularly strong in illustrating the interrelationship of social and legal customs with the monasteries. Both Charles-Edwards and Bitel's works bring the old material found in John Ryan, *Irish Monasticism: Origins and Early Development* (Dublin: Longmans, Green and Co., 1931, rpt. 1981) up to date. Earlier studies such as Gearoid MacNiocaill's *Ireland Before the Vikings* (Dublin: Gill and Macmillan, 1972) and the books of the *doyenne* of early Irish church history, Kathleen Hughes *The Church in Early Irish Society* (Ithaca: Cornell University Press, 1966) and *Early Christian Ireland: Introduction to the Sources* (Ithaca: Cornell University Press, 1972), are still of value in providing a fuller picture of the Ireland of Columbanus' day. H. B. Clarke and Anngret Simms' *The Comparative History of Urban Origins in Non-Roman Europe* (Oxford: BAR International Series 255, 1985) has a section on Ireland that provides much archaeological material for the study of monasteries as population centers. Caitlin Corning's *The Celtic and Roman Traditions: Conflict and Consensus in the Early Medieval Church* (New York: Palgrave Macmillan, 2006) offers an excellent, and understandable, analysis of the points in dispute between the two systems, particularly the Easter Controversy, but in so doing neglects other issues of monastic versus Episcopal authority. As always, Peter Brown's insights on the Irish role in the development of the Western Church contribute much. He devotes an entire chapter of his *The Rise of Western Christendom: Triumph and Diversity, A.D. 200–1000* (Oxford: Blackwell, 1996) to the contributions of Columbanus to the growth of the penitential system.

The Merovingian world that Columbanus encountered is ably described in Edward James' *The Origins of France: From Clovis to the Capetians, 500–1000* (London: Macmillan, 1983) and Patrick J. Geary's novel approach in *Before France and Germany: The Creation and Transformation of the Merovingian World* (Oxford: Oxford University Press, 1988). For Merovingian church matters, J. M. Wallace-Hadrill's *The Frankish Church* (Oxford: Oxford University Press, 1983) is still of use. Ian Wood's fine article "The Vita Columbani and Merovingian Hagiography" *Peritia* 1 (1982), pp. 63–80 offers insights on the reception of Irish penance among the Merovingian bishops. The older study by Henry G. J. Beck, *The Pastoral Care of Souls in South-East France During the Sixth Century* (Rome: Analecta Gregoriana, 1950) remains a treasure trove of information on pre-Columbanian penance. H. B. Clarke and Mary Brennan, eds. *Columbanus and Merovingian Monasticism* (Oxford: BAR International Series 113, 1981) is a collection of essays on the interplay of Merovingian and Irish monasticism. Of particular interest are Ian Wood's "A Prelude to Columbanus: The Monastic Achievement in the Burgundian Territories" (pp. 3–32), which rightly places the monasteries there as congenial candidates for integration into the Columbanian model, and Pierre Riché's, "Columbanus, His Followers, and the Merovingian Church" (pp. 59–72) that points out the appeal of the more ascetic religion that Columbanus offered. For an intriguing analysis of how wandering monks were received in the Merovingian world, see Bernhard Jussen, ed. *Ordering Medieval Society: Perspectives on Intellectual and Practical Modes of Shaping Social Relations* (Philadelphia: University of Pennsylvania Press, 2001). Jussen suggests that Columbanus seemed a threat to Episcopal authority much like the pseudoprophets who peopled late sixth-century Gaul. Steven Fanning's seminal article, "Lombard Arianism Reconsidered," *Speculum 56* 1 (1981), pp. 241–252, was the first to point out that the Lombards, being a composite people, were not as fully Arian as traditionally thought. For Columbanus' lasting influence on his final monastic foundation, Michael Richter's *Bobbio in the Early Middle Ages: The Abiding Legacy of Columbanus* (Dublin: Four Courts Press, 2008) is an insightful and rewarding source.

The collected essays found in Dorothy Whitelock, Rosamond McKitterick, and David Dumville, eds. *Ireland in Early Medieval Europe: Studies in Memory of Kathleen Hughes* (Cambridge: Cambridge University Press, 1982) include an excellent piece by Clare Stancliffe on "Red, White and Blue Martyrdom" (pp. 21–46), as well as Edward James' "Ireland and Western Gaul in the Merovingian Period" (pp. 362–386). For the associated idea of white martyrdom and pilgrimage, one can still turn to Kathleen Hughes' older article, "The Changing Theory and Practice of Irish Pilgrimage" *Journal of Ecclesiastical History* 11 (1960), pp. 143–151. Maribel Dietz's, *Wandering Monks, Virgins, and Pilgrims: Ascetic Travel in the Mediterranean World, A.D. 300–800* (University Park, PA: Pennsylvania State University Press, 2005), brings the finest contemporary research to bear on the concept of pilgrimage during Columbanus' day. The clearest exposition of the differences between life and place pilgrimage is found in Dee Dyas' *Pilgrimage in Medieval English Literature, 700–1500* (Cambridge: D.S. Brewer, 2001).

Dreams and their function in understanding the Late Antique world are treated in Isabel Moreira's *Dreams, Visions, and Spiritual Authority in Merovingian Gaul* (Ithaca: Cornell University Press, 2000). Benedicta Ward's classic study, *Miracles and the Medieval Mind* (Philadelphia: University of Pennsylvania Press, 1987), is supplemented nicely by her collected articles in *Signs and Wonders: Saints, Miracles and Prayer from the 4th Century to the 14th* (Burlington, VT: Ashgate, 1992). Giselle de Nie's considerable body of work on that topic is available in *Word, Image and Experience: Dynamics of Miracle and Self-Perception in Sixth-Century Gaul* (Burlington, VT: Ashgate, 2003). For a concise account of the Late Antique bubonic plague, David Keys' *Catastrophe: An Investigation into the Origins of the Modern World* (New York: Ballantine Books, 1999), while claiming a bit too much for the impact of the plague, is an excellent resource on the mechanics and probable cause of the pandemic. On the notion of Late Antiquity as an historical epoch, one could do no better than to begin with Peter Brown's *The World of Late Antiquity* (London: Thames & Hudson, 1971), the book that started it all. Volumes now proliferate on this topic, but the collection of essays in G. W. Bowersock, Peter Brown, and Oleg Grabar, eds. *Interpreting Late Antiquity: Essays on the Postclassical World* (Cambridge, MA: The Belknap Press of Harvard University, 2001) illustrates well the many ramifications to this realignment of chronology.

Popular works on the world in which Columbanus lived, particularly its Irish sector, have been increasing recently as a by-product of the rise in popularity of all things Celtic. Ted Olsen's *Christianity and the Celts* (Downers Grove, IL: InterVarsity Press, 2003) is a brief, well-written survey, while Thomas Cahill's, *How the Irish Saved Civilization: The Untold Story of Ireland's Heroic Role from the Fall of Rome to the Rise of Medieval Europe* (New York: Anchor Books, 1995) is an exercise in ethnic hyperbole and seems no more than an update of Seumas MacManus' *The Story of the Irish Race: A Popular History of Ireland* (New York: Devin-Adair, 1921), which, it must be noted, remains in print even to this day. A better version of popular history for our period is Carmel McCaffrey and Leo Eaton's *In Search of Ancient Ireland: The Origins of the Irish from Neolithic Times to the Coming of the English* (Chicago: Ivan R. Dee, 2002). Written as a companion piece to the Public Broadcasting System's series of the same name, it has the merit of using the latest archaeological information to adorn its nonethnocentric text.

Major Personalities

Adaloald: (602–628) Son of the Lombard king Agilulf and queen Theudelinda, his birth gave more political and religious leverage to the queen's efforts at converting the people to Catholicism. He reigned for ten years (616–626) after his father's death, but went insane and was deposed by a coalition of nobles.

Agilulf: (r. 590–616) Duke of Turin who was selected, either by the Lombard nobles, Queen Theudelinda, or both, as the successor to the poisoned Authari. He apparently was willing to consider Catholicism, even allowing his son and heir to be baptized as such. During his reign the Lombards extended their power in northern Italy, but did not change from Arianism to Catholicism.

Alboin: (r. 565?–573) King of the Lombards who led his people across the Alps in the spring of 568 for the conquest of much of northern Italy. His victories led to the formation of Lombardy.

Attala: (d. 627) Originally a monk at the southern French island monastery of Lerins, Attala left seeking a more stringent lifestyle and joined Columbanus at Luxeuil. Later accompanying the group on their journey to Bobbio, Attala succeeded to the office of abbot there upon Columbanus' death, and provided Jonas with much information about the life of the founder.

Authari: (c. 540–590) King of the Lombards from 584 until his poisoning in September 590, Authari married the teenage Bavarian princess, Theudelinda, who would play a major role in an attempt to make the Lombards Catholic.

Boniface IV: (c. 550–615) Pope from 608–615, Boniface was the pontiff who received Columbanus' ire in the dispute of The Three Chapters Controversy. Boniface, who was involved in the development of the Church among the barbarian Anglo-Saxons, eventually became a monk himself, dying about six months before Columbanus.

Brunhilda: (c. 550–613) Visigothic princess who was married to Sigebert, Frankish king of Austrasia in 567. The murder of her sister by the royal house of Neustria precipitated a fifty-year feud between her and Fredegund, the consort of Chilperic of Neustria. She became, through her son, grandsons, and great-grandsons, the de facto ruler of, in turn, Austrasia and Burgundy, and was Columbanus' career-long nemesis.

Childebert II: (r. 575–595) Son of Brunhilda and Sigebert and king of Austrasia for twenty years. Upon the death of his uncle, Guntram, in 592, he became ruler of both Austrasia and Burgundy. At first his minority was controlled by the nobles, but later came under the influence of his mother. His sons, Theuderic and Theudebert, became rulers of Burgundy and Austrasia upon his death.

Chilperic: (r. 561–584) Son of Chlotar I and grandson of the great Clovis, Chilperic was King of Neustria. His concubine and later queen, Fredegund, instigated his dismissal of his wife, the murder of his second bride, and the ultimate hostilities that divided the Merovingian world from 567 through 613. He was assassinated in 584 at Chelles. His son, Chlotar II, eventually reunited Gaul under his rule.

Chlotar I: (r. 511–561) Son of Clovis, Chlotar managed to unite Gaul in the last six years of his life. He left behind four sons, who partitioned the lands among themselves and continued the cycle of violence that plagued the Merovingian royal house.

Chlotar II: (r. 584–629) Son of Chilperic and Fredegund, Chlotar put an end to the long-running royal feud by executing Brunhilda in 613, thereby uniting Gaul. He was a generally dependable friend of Columbanus, even offering shelter to him in trying times as well as supporting his monastic foundations.

Columba: (521–597) Irish saint and missionary, Columba was of royal lineage and, chagrined by his involvement in a civil war, an early practitioner of white martyrdom. He is credited with converting the Picts and the foundation of the significant monastery at the island known as Iona.

Comgall: (516–602) Founder of the great Irish monastic center at Bangor, Comgall was the son of a soldier and a great believer in asceticism. His approach was mimicked in the continental foundations of Columbanus.

Croine Beag: Mysterious anchoress who reputedly lived in the vicinity of the modern Irish town of Carlow, she is credited with persuading the young Columbanus to forsake the world and enter a monastery (c. 558–560).

Finnian of Clonard: (c. 470–548) A native Leinsterman like Columbanus, Finnian founded the great monastery at *Cluain Erard*, or "high meadow," around 520. It became an incubator for many who went on to establish significant monasteries in Ireland. His model of asceticism became the basis for much of Irish monastic practice.

Fredegund: (d. 596) Lowborn consort to Chilperic, the king of Neustria. Fredegund apparently had such a hold over the king that she got him to renounce his first wife, Audovera, and later kill his Visigothic bride. Her actions are blamed for beginning a royal feud between the houses of Austrasia and Neustria that disrupted Merovingian society for nearly fifty years.

Gall: (c. 551–646) One of the original companions of Columbanus, Gall was gifted in language acquisition and spearheaded the missions effort among the Germanic tribes around Lake Constance. Even though he split with Columbanus over this, his efforts were crowned with the eventual founding of St. Gallen, one of the most influential monasteries in medieval Europe.

Gregory of Tours: (538–594) Bishop of Tours, 573–594, Gregory was the chief custodian of the St. Martin cult, and one of the most influential historians of the sixth-century period.

Guntram: (r. 561–592) One of the four sons of Chlotar I, Guntram reigned as king of Burgundy for more than thirty years. Lacking heirs, he became the uncle protector to a series of nephews and was instrumental in the survival of the Merovingian royal line. He appears to have been the monarch that Columbanus first approached when he arrived in Gaul.

Jonas of Bobbio: (c. 600–659) Born in the Piedmont at Susa, Jonas entered the monastery of Bobbio in 618 and soon became secretary to the abbot, Attala. He worked in missions in modern-day Belgium and northern France and composed a life of St. Vaast, the Frankish bishop of Arras. On a visit to Bobbio in 639, he committed to write a life of Columbanus, which he completed by 642/643.

Leoparius: Bishop of Tours who succeeded Gregory in 594, Leoparius offered hospitality to Columbanus and his party on their exile voyage down the Loire River.

Martin of Tours: (c. 316–397) Monastic founder and bishop of Tours from 372–397, Martin became the preeminent saint in the Late Antique west. His life, recorded by Sulpicius Severus, served as the model for saints' lives ever after and the miracles performed at his tomb were so profuse as to cause Gregory of Tours to write a four-volume work on them.

Paul the Deacon: (c. 720–800) Born of a noble Lombard family, Paul became first a deacon, as his title implies, then a monk, finishing his days at the great Benedictine Abbey of Monte Cassino. He was the first to attempt a history of his people, the renowned *History of the Lombards*, written sometime after 787. Among his other works was the first extant history of an Episcopal see, *The History of the Bishops of Metz.*

Sigebert: (r. 561–575) One of the four sons of Chlotar I, Sigebert ruled in Austrasia. His marriage to the Visigothic princess Brunhilda in 567 set in motion events that led to the vicious Merovingian royal feud. He was assassinated at Vitry in 575, probably at the instigation of Fredegund and Chilperic. His five-year-old son, Childebert II, ruled the kingdom under the supervision of Brunhilda until 595.

Sinell: (fl. 540s–560s) Founder of the monastery at Cleenish, where Columbanus first became a monk. Sinell had studied under St. Finnian at Clonard and left to found his own monastery upon Finnian's death in 548.

Theudebert: (587–612) Grandson of Brunhilda and king of Austrasia (595–612), Theudebert at first supported and then opposed his grandmother's plans for rule. He was defeated in battle by Brunhilda and Theuderic at Zulpich, and soon after executed.

Theudelinda: (c. 570–628) Daughter of Garibald, Duke of Bavaria, Theudelinda was wed first to the Lombard King Authari, then, upon his assassination, to his successor Agilulf. Theudelinda was allowed to choose her new husband and next monarch. Since she was a staunch Catholic, she worked effectively to move the Lombards away from Arianism. Her support of Columbanus was key in his success at Bobbio. She remained the power behind the throne during the decade of her son Adaloald's reign.

Theuderic: (589–613) Grandson of Brunhilda and king of Burgundy (r. 595–613), Theuderic also briefly reigned as king of both Austrasia and Burgundy after his victory over his brother, Theudebert. His death by dysentery, in 613, began the series of events that would lead to Brunhilda's downfall. His heirs, born of concubines rather than legitimate wives, were the point of contention between the Burgundian royal house and Columbanus.

The Merovingians of Columbanus' Day

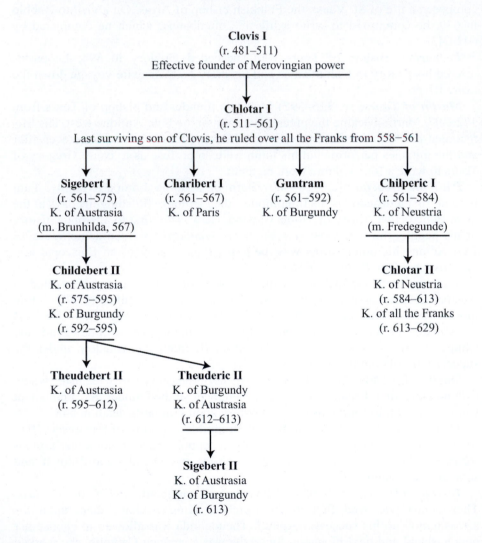

Clovis I
(r. 481–511)
Effective founder of Merovingian power

Chlotar I
(r. 511–561)
Last surviving son of Clovis, he ruled over all the Franks from 558–561

Sigebert I
(r. 561–575)
K. of Austrasia
(m. Brunhilda, 567)

Charibert I
(r. 561–567)
K. of Paris

Guntram
(r. 561–592)
K. of Burgundy

Chilperic I
(r. 561–584)
K. of Neustria
(m. Fredegunde)

Childebert II
K. of Austrasia
(r. 575–595)
K. of Burgundy
(r. 592–595)

Chlotar II
K. of Neustria
(r. 584–613)
K. of all the Franks
(r. 613–629)

Theudebert II
K. of Austrasia
(r. 595–612)

Theuderic II
K. of Burgundy
K. of Austrasia
(r. 612–613)

Sigebert II
K. of Austrasia
K. of Burgundy
(r. 613)

Glossary

Anamchara: "Soul-friend"; the Irish monastic practice of pairing up monks for accountability and spiritual support.

Annegray: Old *Anagrates*, this was the first monastic foundation established by Columbanus in the Vosges Mountains of Burgundy.

Anchoress (**Anchorite**): A female (or male) who opted for a life of solitude in worship of God.

Arianism: The belief that God the Father preceded God the Son, named after Arius (d. 336). Seemingly condemned at the Council of Nicaea in 325, throughout much of the fourth century, Arianism went in and out of favor in the Roman Imperial court. During this time some barbarian tribes were converted to this form or Christianity, creating further conflict when they invaded the Empire. The theological problem in Arianism was that Christ, if a created being, could not be truly God, who is uncreated.

Austrasia: The northeastern section of Gaul and a major kingdom within the Merovingian royal partition. Upon the death of Clovis in 511, his four sons divided up Gaul, thus creating a section called Austrasia. It continued as a separate kingdom except during those rare times when one monarch could unite the whole of Gaul. Austrasia suffered from its proximity to the barbarian peoples living just beyond the Rhine, who were alternately useful and threatening to royal ambitions.

Bangor: A key Irish monastery founded by Comgall (c. 558), it was the monastic home of Columbanus for some thirty years. The form of penance that came to be known as *Irish* or *tariffed* flowed from Bangor to the rest of Europe.

Blackstairs Mountains: Mountain range in southeastern Ireland within the old kingdom of Leinster. Columbanus was apparently born somewhere on the eastern side of these mountains.

Blot: Germanic concept that the king should stand before the gods on behalf of his people. In practice, this concept meant that any king straying from traditional religion would run the risk of angering the whole people and could be subject to deposition.

Bobbio: Old Bobium in the Trebbia Valley of the Appenines, this site was given to Columbanus by the Lombard King Agilulf for the foundation of a monastery. Bobbio became a leading monastery and had great cultural impact throughout the Middle Ages. One of its abbots, Gerbert, became Pope Sylvester II

(r. 999–1003), considered to be a leading figure in widening Europe's intellectual heritage.

Bog: Wetlands in Ireland composed of rotting vegetation, they comprise about one seventh of the island and produce peat, a principal source of fuel. They posed a natural barrier to travel in the Middle Ages.

Bot: Germanic legal concept that held that each crime had an equivalent physical punishment.

Boothies: The small huts of wattle and daub, or sometimes stone, constructed by Irish monks to house their community. Rather than using a dormitory-style approach, the monks built many of these small shelters to house two or three at a time.

Bregenz: Old Roman *Brigantia* on the eastern shore of Lake Constance, Bregenz was the site of Columbanus' settlement during his efforts to convert the Germans. Gall remained there when Columbanus left and later founded a monastery nearby.

Burgundy: Originally a separate kingdom established by the invading Germanic tribe of Burgundians in the fifth century, by 534, Burgundy had been conquered by the Franks. It then became a kingdom within the Merovingian royal patrimony, subject to rule by whichever king could claim it. During Columbanus' day, Burgundy was ruled by Guntram (r. 561–592), Childebert II (r. 592–595), and Theuderic (r. 595–613).

Cenobitic Monasticism: Group monasticism involving a community of monks or nuns working together to worship God by their efforts.

Chalon-sur-Saône: City in Burgundy on the Saône River, in 602, it was the site of a church council that was called to discipline Columbanus for his unwillingness to come under Episcopal control.

Clausura: The enclosed or restricted part of the Irish monastery. This section was off limits to all but the monks, thereby creating tension when royals or other church dignitaries demanded entrance.

Cleenish: (*Cluain Inis*, or "meadow isle") Monastery founded by Sinell on an island in Lower Lough Erne sometime after 548. This was Columbanus' first monastic home and the location of his primary academic training.

Clonard: Old *Cluain Erard*, or "high meadow," Clonard was the site of St. Finnian's famous monastery. When Finnian died of the plague in 548, several great monastic founders dispersed from Clonard to dot Ireland with their foundations.

Curragh: Irish seagoing vessel of the early Middle Ages, it was a frame boat covered in waterproofed hides.

Domus Ecclesiae: The "household of the Church," an alternative to the secular *domus familiaque* or family household, this was an attempt to invest the bishop with a paternalistic function for those in his diocese. Bishops were expected to care for the poor and provide protection to their "family."

Dun: The Irish family homestead that included an extended kindred, as well as lands and buildings, it functioned as a type of social and political base for the clan.

Eremitic Monasticism: Individual- or "hermit"-style monasticism. Eremitic monasticism was often the original form of that endeavor, frequently morphing into group or cenobitic monasticism.

Esker: Gravel ridges that traverse Ireland presumably as a result of Ice Age glacial deposits. Eskers provided natural trackways through difficult terrain and were thus seen as primitive roads. Evidence points to the inhabitants of Ireland improving and in some cases covering with planking many of these eskers as early as the fourth millennium B.C.

Fer Leighann: The master instructor in the Irish monasteries. During the first years of monasticism, the actual founder of the monastery often filled this role.

Fine: The Irish family, it encompassed blood relations of an extended nature. The fine provided protection for its members in this age before centralized government.

Fontaines: Third monastery founded in the Vosges by Columbanus. It too was a deserted, previously occupied, site called *Fontanas*. The proximity of the three Burgundian monasteries, Annegray, Luxeuil, and Fontaines, made them easy for Columbanus to oversee.

Gaul: Major section of Western Europe that encompassed modern-day France, parts of Switzerland, and Belgium. Named after the Celtic tribes that had gained dominance over the area sometime in the sixth or fifth century B.C. These Gallic tribesmen posed such a threat to Rome that Julius Caesar felt it necessary to conquer them in the 50s B.C., and Gaul became a fundamental part of the Roman Empire.

Glas: An Irish word meaning "blue," or "green," or "blue-green," or even "pale." This became the term for a second type of martyrdom aside from dying for the faith. In *glas* martyrdom, the individual would separate himself or herself from society and live a life of renunciation in the wilderness.

Hagiography: "Holy writing." Hagiography is the committing to story form the workings of God through His saints. It is not true history in that the wondrous is emphasized, often at the expense of facts, and details that do not add to the general purpose of spiritual edification are passed over.

Iona: Originally just "*insula*," or island, Iona was the site of the most famous monastery established by St. Columba (521–597). In later years it was also called *Hi* and became a model for Irish monasteries outside of Ireland.

Justinian's Plague: A pandemic of bubonic plague that began during the reign of the Emperor Justinian (527–565). Possibly triggered by disturbances as far away as modern-day Indonesia, the plague traveled via fleas and rats. The first European manifestation began in 541, and it continued to pulse through the population well into the early eighth century.

Late Antiquity/Late Antique: An historical designation made popular by Peter Brown in the 1970s, it reorders the break between the ancient and medieval worlds to include a period encompassing the last centuries of the Roman Empire and the first centuries of the postinvasion era (c. A.D. 150–750).

Leinster: Southeastern kingdom in Ireland and the birthplace of Columbanus.

Lombardy: Territory in northern Italy conquered in 568 and thereafter by the last great Germanic tribe to invade the western half of the Roman Empire, the Lombards. The kingdom they set up was somewhat territorially fluid, depending on Byzantine power, but was eventually conquered by Charlemagne and made a part of his empire. The principal city in Lombardy was Milan, although the Lombards used Pavia as their capital.

Lough Erne: A lake in northwestern Ireland, Lower Lough Erne was the site of Columbanus' first monastic affiliation at Cleenish.

Luxeuil: The second monastery founded in the Vosges by Columbanus, it was an old fortified settlement called *Luxovium* that had been destroyed by Attila and the Huns in 451. Luxeuil became, along with Bobbio, the most famous of the Columbanian houses during the Middle Ages.

Martyrdom: The loss of one's life for the faith. The Irish took the concept beyond physical death and developed two other forms of martyrdom involving voluntary exile in the wilderness and voluntary permanent exile from the homeland.

Merovingians: The royal house among the Franks from the fourth through the eighth centuries. Named after an early king, Meroveus, the Merovingians were said to have a family trait that included long blond hair. Their inheritance policies encouraged much intrafamilial strife.

Milan: Old Roman *Mediolanum*, Milan was a major city in the Roman Empire. In 286, the Emperor Diocletian made Milan one of the four capitals in his newly reorganized Roman government. It became a principal location of Western history and was the site of Constantine's edict of toleration for Christianity. Its bishop, Ambrose (340–397), was the ranking prelate in the West of his day and acted as a tutor to the great Church father, Augustine. In Columbanus' day, the Lombards controlled Milan, although their capital was actually Pavia to the south. The rich heritage of religion in Milan only added to the deep divisions that existed there concerning The Three Chapters Controversy.

Miracula: "Miracle." The supernatural suspension of the natural order. This word was less frequently used in Columbanus' day in lieu of the word *signum,* or sign.

Monophysites: Those who followed the teachings of Cyril, Patriarch of Alexandria (412–444), that Christ was of "one substance" only—the Divine— hence the word *monophysite*, or "mono-physis."

Muinter: The Irish word for "family," derived from the word for monastery. It came to replace the word *fine*, signifying how much the monastic world was influencing secular society in Ireland.

Natalicia: "Birthday poems" made popular by Paulinus of Nola (354–431). Paulinus wrote these poems to commemorate St. Felix of Nola on the anniversary of his spiritual "birthday," which was the day of his death.

Neustria: One of the kingdoms of Merovingian Gaul. Neustria was the central portion of the land, with its capital at Soissons. During Columbanus' day, Neustria was ruled by Chlotar II (584–629), the son of Chilperic and Fredegund. Chlotar II used his base in Neustria to eventually conquer and unify the rest of Gaul in 613.

Pavia: Originally *Ticinum*, a city on the Ticino River, Pavia was chosen to be the Lombard capital due to its more defensible site. Pavia served as the Lombard capital until Charlemagne conquered the territory in 774.

Peace-Weaver: A Germanic kenning, or symbolic term, a peace-weaver was a bride married to a groom from an opposing kindred or kingdom. The objective was to "weave peace" between to warring parties via marriage. Generally the "peace-weaver" had little or no say in both the wedding and the subsequent marriage.

Peccata Capitalia: Capital or deadly sins. These transgressions required the full treatment of public penance, without which the subject would be condemned to hell. Once penance was done for these sins, no repeat reconciliation was possible.

Peccata Minuta: Lesser or smaller sins. These transgressions, while still serious, could be atoned for by private acts of penance. The penitent could do penance repeatedly for these sins.

Peregrinus (Alither): "Pilgrim" in Latin and Irish. The earlier meaning of the term was that of "outcast," in that the pilgrim was to leave his or her society permanently. Later, the word came to signify one who traveled to and returned from a specific destination with a spiritual benefit.

Praepositus: A position of monastic leadership, the praepositus was a type of under-abbot over a monastery affiliated with a larger foundation.

Reverentia: "Reverence." Term used for the full belief in the efficacy of the saints.

Rusticitas: "Rusticity." Term used for those who did not believe in saints' power. The term alludes to the general tendency of the country folk to resist Christianization in the first centuries of the Church.

Scramasax: A single-edged large knife used by the Germanic peoples particularly in England and France. The fuller, or groove in the blade, was often smeared with poison to ensure that wounds inflicted by this weapon would be fatal. It was a favorite choice of assassins during this period.

Signum: "Sign," used to describe what we would consider miracles. The implication was that the *signum* was a confirmation of holiness, and not the unusual intervention of God into the normal order of things.

Slige (Sliged): "Cuttings," in Irish. A term used to describe the primitive roadways of ancient Ireland. These often followed animal pathways, or natural formations, and were reinforced by the use of oak planking.

Tariffed Penance: The Irish form of penance, possibly developed at Bangor, that was repeatable, and offered a correlation between the sin and the appropriate penance.

Temeritas: Audacity, or temerity. A code word used in the sources of the sixth and seventh centuries describing one who did not believe in the efficacy of the saints.

The Three Chapters Controversy: A theological dispute that disturbed the peace of the Church from the 540s until the end of the seventh century. The controversy turned on the relative orthodoxy of three pieces of theological writing, hence the name *Three Chapters*. Theodore of Mopsuestia, Theodoret of Cyrrhus, and Ibas of Edessa were condemned as "Nestorians" (those who did not fully recognize the divinity of Christ) and declared heretics by the command of the Emperor Justinian (r. 527–565). The problem was that the Council of Chalcedon had not condemned all three, but only Theodore, so the move by Justinian was seen as condemning not just heretics but an officially called and sanctioned general council of the Church. Consequently the argument turned on very fine points of doctrine and was settled only when the pope ruled that the council had done the right thing.

Troscud: The Irish custom of protest fasting. This hunger strike was designed to embarrass, and thus defeat, the opponent.

Vallum: The ditch and wooden-spiked barrier around an Irish monastery. The purpose was to mark the boundary, keep out wild beasts, and prevent unauthorized persons from entering.

Virtus: Late Antique religious word for "holy deeds." The implication of *virtus* was that it signified what God was able to do through His saints, not what they could do in their own power.

Index